An Authentic Narrative of the Proceedings of the Expedition under the Command of Brigadier-Gen. Craufurd; until its arrival at Monte-Video; with an account of the operations against Buenos Ayres under the command of Lieut.-Gen. Whitelocke.

Robert Craufurd, John Whitelocke

An Authentic Narrative of the Proceedings of the Expedition under the Command of Brigadier-Gen. Craufurd; until its arrival at Monte-Video; with an account of the operations against Buenos Ayres under the command of Lieut.-Gen. Whitelocke. By an Officer of the Expedition [i.e. John Whitelocke]. [With plates, including maps.]

Craufurd, Robert
British Library, Historical Print Editions
British Library
1808 [1807]
viii, 216 p. ; 8°.
9781.d.11.

GUIDE TO FOLD-OUTS, MAPS and OVERSIZED IMAGES

In an online database, page images do not need to conform to the size restrictions found in a printed book. When converting these images back into a printed bound book, the page sizes are standardized in ways that maintain the detail of the original. For large images, such as fold-out maps, the original page image is split into two or more pages.

Guidelines used to determine the split of oversize pages:

• Some images are split vertically; large images require vertical and horizontal splits.
• For horizontal splits, the content is split left to right.
• For vertical splits, the content is split from top to bottom.
• For both vertical and horizontal splits, the image is processed from top left to bottom right.

AUTHENTIC NARRATIVE

OF THE

Proceedings of the Expedition

UNDER THE COMMAND OF

BRIGADIER-GEN. CRAUFURD;

UNTIL ITS ARRIVAL AT MONTE VIDEO;

WITH AN ACCOUNT OF THE

OPERATIONS AGAINST BUENOS AYRES

UNDER THE COMMAND OF

Lieut.-Gen. Whitelocke.

BY AN OFFICER OF THE EXPEDITION.

LONDON:

PRINTED FOR THE AUTHOR,

AND

SOLD AT No. 18, CHAPEL PLACE, OXFORD CHAPEL.

1808.

ERRATA.

Page. Line.

8, last, erase *s* in *quarters*.

44, 21, *for* conveyed, *read* convoyed.

54, 1, rivetted, revetted.

72, 2, wind, winds.

82, 21, winds, wind.

103, 3, rivetted, revetted.

104, 3, feet, paces.

137, 6, reserve, reverse.

148, 15, leizure, leisure.

162, 26, intention, attention.

187, 3, are, is.

193, 6, in, on.

201, last, it, them.

206, 7, divisions, division.

G. E. MILLS, Printer, 127, Oxford Street.

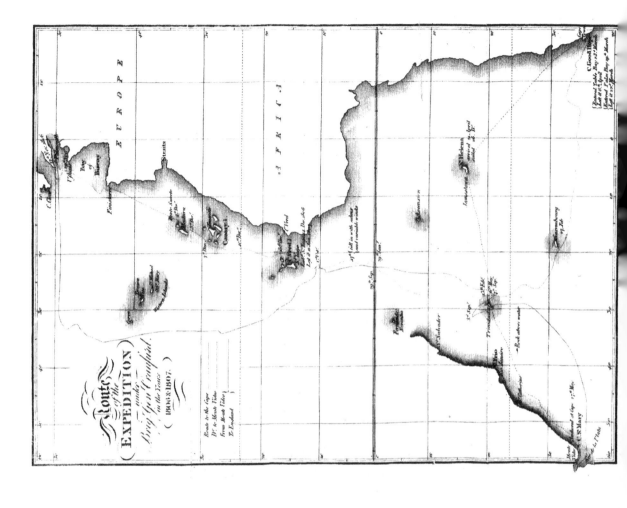

ADVERTISEMENT.

An English Gentleman left in a diplomatic capacity by the Commander of the Forces, at Buenos Ayres, *and every way qualified for such an undertaking, intends giving to the Public, an Historical Work, of the Spanish Vice-royalties in* South America. *To assist him in this undertaking he has had access to libraries in* Buenos Ayres *containing documents, which have never yet been consulted by those who have hitherto written on the subject; and he has met with no little aid from some liberal and well enlightened clergymen, in possession of manuscripts from the different missionaries employed over the Continent. From the acknowledged learning and talents of the Author it cannot be doubted, but that the intended publication will be the most complete respecting* South America, *which has yet met the eye of the Naturalist and Historian.*

PREFACE.

The following narrative was originally written to contribute towards passing over the tediousness incidental to long voyages, as well as for the amusement of the writer's friends; and not intended for the public. Events have, however, determined him upon following the advice of those who, having perused the manuscript, recommended it to him to send it to the press.

A much stronger motive than the little vanity of becoming a journalist, has had a large share in making him adopt such a determination. It is that of *duty towards his companions in arms*, who require to have laid before the public circumstantial details of the operations against *Buenos Ayres*, that the imputation may not attach to them, of having disgraced the British Army by being defective in those qualities which constitute the character of its soldiers. In attempting to fulfil this duty, he is conscious of not having wilfully departed from facts, although he admits of the possibility of having been mis-led by information, in some instances: but having been an eye witness of the most important events recorded in this narrative, he is certain of having stated them correctly. The observations on the failure of the attack, and the apparent causes, certainly arise from a strong feeling of the disgrace and injury brought upon every individual concerned; but in the justice of these remarks, he is equally certain of being supported by the voice of his fellow-soldiers.

The narrative is divided into two parts. The first cannot add much to the information already in possession, from the accounts of men better calculated to give professional remarks on the voyages to, as well as historical descriptions of, the countries visited by General Craufurd's expedition. But having felt, in common with his messmates, the want of a work which would have assisted them much in their expectations of winds, weather, and other circumstances on which the voyage depended, he thought this might, in some degree, obviate a similar difficulty with other young travellers pursuing the same tracks. The second part is confined to the transactions in *South America,* during the short period the British troops had a footing in it.

As the writer has not come before the public to acquire literary fame, but for the reasons assigned above, it was not considered immediately necessary to communicate his name. Should, however, occasion demand it, he will not hesitate to maintain the truth of the narrative by an open avowal of himself.

It is to be hoped, that the style of the production will be received with indulgence, as a soldier has other duties to attend to besides the study of embellished language.

CONTENTS.

Page.

CHAPTER I.] *Preparations for Departure from* Falmouth 1

CHAPTER II.] *Departure from* Falmouth.—*Entrance into the Tropical Seas* ······························· 8

CHAPTER III.] *Arrival at* St. Jago.—*Occurrences there, and Departure* ······························· 17

CHAPTER IV.] *Description of* Porto Praya, *with some Account of its Inhabitants* ····················· 27

CHAPTER V.] *Passage to the* Cape of Good Hope.— *Occurrences there, and Departure for* St. Helena······ 35

CHAPTER VI.] *Some Account of the* Cape Settlement···· 50

CHAPTER VII.] *Continuation of the Description* ······ 64

CHAPTER VIII.] *Passage to and Arrival at* St. Helena. —*Some Account of the Island*···················· 73

CHAPTER IX.] *Departure from* St. Helena.—*Passage across the* South Atlantic, *and Arrival at* Monte Video, *in the* Rio de la Plata····························· 81

PART II.

CHAPTER I.] *Brief Account of the Transactions against* General Beresford, *after the Capture of* Buenos Ayres *in* 1806.—*Arrival of Reinforcements from the* Cape *and from* England.—*Advance of these against* Monte Video 93

Page.

CHAPTER II.] *Description of the Town of* Monte Video.
—*Assault.*—*Transactions from this Period until the
Arrival of General Craufurd's Army* •••••••••••• 102

CHAPTER III.] *Preparations to sail against* Buenos
Ayres.—*Departure from* Monte Video.—*Arrival at*
Colonia del Sacramento.—*Landing at* Ensenada.—
March from thence to Reduction. •••••••••••••• 115

CHAPTER IV.] *Passage over the* Chieulo.—*Action of
the Evening of the 2d July.*—*Transactions during the
3d and 4th* •••••••••••••••••• : •••••••••• 128

CHAPTER V.] *Description of* Buenos Ayres, *and Account
of the Preparations made for its Defence* •••••••• 141

CHAPTER VI.] *Assault of* Buenos Ayres, *on the 5th of
July* ••••••••••••••••••••••••••••••••••• 149

CHAPTER VII.] *Transactions in Consequence of the Issue
of the Attack.*—*Observations thereon* ••••••••••• 166

CHAPTER VIII.] *Some Account of the Country, and of
the Manners and Customs of its Inhabitants* •••••••• 182

CHAPTER IX.] *Description continued.*—*Remarks on the
Political Disposition of the People, and on the probable
Effects of the Invasion to* Great Britain *and the
American Spaniards* ••••••••••••••••••••••• 193

CHAPTER X.] *Thanks returned to the Army in General
Orders.*—*Disorders arising from the Fatigues of the
Army.*—*Arrival, at* Monte Video, *of the Spanish
Hostages, also of the 89th Infantry.*—*Proclamation,
and Remarks thereon.*—*Departure of the First Division
for* England •••••••••••••••••••••••••••••• 205

NARRATIVE,

&c. &c. &c.

CHAPTER I.

Preparations for Departure from Falmouth.

EARLY in the summer of 1806, the persons administering the government of *Great Britain* embarked large detachments of troops in the various ports along the *Channel*, to be employed in services required by the particular circumstances arising during the course of hostilities, which were becoming general in every quarter of the globe. It appeared to be the particular object of this administration to direct the armed force of the country against the colonies of the allies of *France*, through whom a great part of her revenues were drawn for carrying on her measures of aggrandizement on the continent of *Europe*. The peculiarly unhappy situation of the King of

Naples rendered it necessary to send reinforcements to the *Mediterranean*, that we might be enabled to assist in securing to this monarch the Island of *Sicily*, which now remained his only possession, in consequence of the invasion of his continental territory by the French. A large part of the force afloat was therefore immediately dispatched for this purpose, and many regiments remained embarked, without any apparent object for them to be directed at. They were not, however, long in this state, before a new field was opened to give them a career likely to be attended with glory to themselves, and the production of the greatest advantages to the commercial interest of the country; while a blow would be struck at the enemy, more severe than he had felt in the course of a century past.

Dispatches had arrived in April, with an account of the capture of the colony of the *Cape of Good Hope*, by the expedition under Sir David Baird and Sir Home Popham, which had left *England* in the summer of 1805. In August further dispatches reached *England*, signed by Sir Home Popham and General Beresford, dated from *Buenos Ayres*, the capital of the viceroyalty so named, in *South America*, against which they had sailed from the *Cape of Good*

Hope, by order of Sir David Baird. The capture of this city, with so small a force as these commanders had brought against it, excited much triumph in the British dominions; and although an act unauthorized on the part of government, yet it appeared inclined to take advantage of this unexpected conquest, to cut off from *Spain* the most valuable part of her possessions in the new world, as well as to open a new channel for the disposal of the manufactures of the country, which were crowding the English warehouses, in consequence of the steps taken by Buonaparté to prevent their circulation through any part of the Continent, where his influence predominated. Great expectations were held out on this subject by Sir Home Popham's dispatches, and public letters addressed to the *London* merchants; and Sir Home Popham's knowledge of the commercial concerns of the country was held in very high estimation.

Notwithstanding the preparation in which the troops had been kept ready for sea, it was not until the 11th of October that Brigadier-General Sir Samuel Auchmuty sailed with reinforcements to General Beresford: he had under his command the 17th Dragoons, 40th and 87th Regiments of Infantry, with three companies of the Rifle Corps.

There now remained in port several regiments of infantry, and they were ordered on a service, which, from the mystery in which it became involved, excited in no small degree the curiosity and speculations of all parties. They rendezvoused at *Falmouth*, and when united composed a very respectable force, consisting of

Two squadrons 6th Dragoon Guards.

5th
36th
45th } Regiments of Infantry.
88th

Five companies of the Rifle Corps.

Two companies of the Royal Artillery.

The transports, on board of which these troops had been embarked, were particularly selected by the Transport Board as best calculated for their comfort during a long period: such as were not coppered at first, were ordered to be sheathed with this metal expressly for this service; and every preparation made, denoted the expedition to be remote, or expected to be of long duration. The conjectures on this head were various; but that respecting the commencement of our operations at *Vera Cruz*, in the *Gulph of Mexico*, appeared to be founded on the best reasoning: at all events, there appeared little doubt but that some part of the Spanish possessions in *America* was to become the theatre of our military operations.

To command this little army Colonel Robert Craufurd had been nominated through the interest of Mr. Windham, the war minister of the day. The unprecedented circumstance of a colonel (and nearly the junior of his rank) being appointed to a command fit for a lieutenant-general, excited much opposition to Mr. Windham's nomination, and loud murmurs on the part of those officers of superior rank who remained unemployed; but the firmness of the Secretary of the War Department succeeded, and Colonel Craufurd (raised to the rank of brigadier on the occasion) afterwards proved himself, as far as he came into action, in every respect worthy the high opinion entertained of his talents and qualifications by his patron. He had a large staff attached to his command; and every appearance denoted it to be independent of any other. It would have been a happy circumstance for this little army, had it not afterwards fallen under the authority of any other person.

The troops were lying in *Falmouth* some time previous to the arrival of General Craufurd, which did not take place until the morning of the 24th

of October. The first order which he issued
related to such officers as had embarked their
families. In a circular letter on the occasion, he
observed that motives of humanity towards the
ladies themselves, as well as the view of securing
the utmost comfort to the officers embarked,
rendered it necessary that the married gentlemen
should order their wives on shore, who would
otherwise remain exposed to suffer severe hardships, during a service, of the nature of which he
was the most competent judge. It was certainly
to be lamented that such an order had not been
originally issued, if always intended, as the officers
with families had expended much of their pay in
advance to provide for their comforts during a
long voyage; and now they became burthened
with the additional travelling expences for the
removal of their wives and children to a place of
protection near their friends, as well as to raise
a fund for their separate maintenance. It will be
but doing justice to General Craufurd to add,
that however cruel this measure was considered at
the moment, those concerned felt the advantages
of it at a future period.

The General suddenly left *Falmouth* for
London on the 26th. This occasioned some
surprise, and indeed some uneasiness on the part

of the troops, who were afraid that the expedition might possibly be countermanded. It was not until his return to join it on the 2d of November that this sensation subsided. He visited the different transports, examined narrowly into their condition, inspected minutely the appearance of every man embarked, and gave liberal orders for providing every article which commanding officers deemed fit to add to the comfort of the soldiers. The troops were in the highest state of bodily health, a circumstance reflecting the greatest credit on the officers, as some had been on board, with very little intermission, since the 26th of July.

We were now in a complete state of preparation, and waiting only for a fair wind to proceed on our course: it had almost constantly blown from the S.W. and the advanced season of the year rendered us anxious to clear the *Channel* as early as possible. On the 11th, the wind hauled round to the N.E. and the signal to prepare for sailing was hoisted on board the Commodore; but as it did not blow sufficiently strong to take out the men of war, we did not get under weigh until the next morning.

CHAPTER II.

Departure from Falmouth.—*Entrance into the Tropical Seas.*

I<small>T</small> was near three in the afternoon of the 12th before the whole convoy could get out, when it amounted to forty sail, including some transports with the 9th Dragoons on board, and several merchantmen for *Buenos Ayres.* We sailed under the protection of four seventy-fours, one frigate, two gun-brigs, and two schooners, under the command of the Honorable Captain Stopford, of the Spencer, on board of which had likewise embarked General Craufurd. It was not intended that these men of war should accompany us beyond a certain latitude, when we were to be joined by Admiral Murray, with several sixty-four gun ships, and under whom was to be placed the naval part of the expedition.

The wind continued fair, but light, until the 14th, when it came round to the S.W. obliging the fleet to stand W.N.W. This day the Juliana transport, the head-quarters ship of the 36th, appeared without her mizen mast, and main-top gallant mast, both of which had been carried away the preceding night by the Captain, seventy-four; the crew of which were giving every assistance to replace these losses. Another ship of the convoy had like to have shared a similar fate from the Nereide frigate, whose Commander, from a *too strict adherence* to naval etiquette, run on board a large transport, standing in a different tack: fortunately, there was but little wind or sea at the time, or the consequences might have proved more serious than the loss of a jib-boom and sprit sail yard to the frigate, without injuring the transport.

During this night we lost eleven sail of the fleet, owing to their not having observed the signal made to put about. They hove in sight again about noon, and rejoined convoy.

The wind still continued unfavorable, and on the 19th came on to blow very strong, accompanied with a very heavy sea. Several of the ships had part of their sails and rigging carried away, and they were obliged to make every thing snug, to encounter a gale which appeared to threaten us. Our preparations were not thrown away, as it blew most violently, with little intermission until the 22d, when both wind and sea

C

moderated. It continued, however, to blow from the same unfavorable point, but with clear weather, until the 29th, when it came from the N.N.W. We had spoke during this time with several ships of the convoy, and learnt from the Campion store-ship, that she had sprung a leak during the gale, and at one time had in her hold above five feet water; they had the good fortune to discover the leak, and to receive assistance from the Captain, seventy-four, or she must inevitably have foundered. The Nereide frigate and a merchantman had left us in the storm, nor could the absence of the former be accounted for by the other men of war. We were this day fifteen leagues to the westward of *Cape Finisterre.*

The comforts of a fair wind and fine weather were now experienced, and we sailed on at a brisk rate, till the afternoon of the 4th December, when the signal was made for land being in sight to the W.S.W. which proved to be *Porto Sancto.* A store-ship and brig, under the charge of two small armed vessels, were sent forward to *Madeira:* the Commissary-general of the expedition went in with them, to obtain wine for the use of the troops. Lemon juice and sugar were now issued to the men.

We lay to on the 5th December, about seven leagues to the southward of *Madeira*, during which time the vessels communicated with each other. A report was now in circulation among them, that it was intended to attack the Island of *Teneriffe;* and although the information came from one of the Captains of the line-of-battle ships, and also from an agent, yet it met with little credit. It could not be easily imagined that such mighty preparations as had been made in favor of the expedition, should only have in view the possession of an island, by which we would be as little benefited, as our enemies would be injured in losing it. It was not easier to reconcile the idea of risking the ultimate object of the expedition, by attempting a *coup-de-main* on a place which had been proved, during the last war, to be not totally defenceless.

While laying to, a dead sun-fish of immense bulk passed close alongside the ship: it had the appearance of the flayed carcase of some large quadruped. One of the seamen struck a boat-hook into it, without being able to draw it out, or raise the fish. A boat was lowered, and this lump of blubber was attempted to be hoisted in, but it had not consistency sufficient to support its own weight, and it dropped into several pieces, some of which we saved to serve as bait for dolphins, which were in the train of this sun-fish in great numbers. We hooked several, but only succeeded in killing two, which being stewed in wine for the next day's dinner, were much relished. It is worthy of remark, that no other vessel of the fleet saw any dolphins on the passage to *St. Jago*, nor did we observe any others than those in the train of the sun-fish.

In the evening we continued our course to the southward with a very strong gale after us, and we could carry but little sail. The fleet laboured severely; but as the wind was fair, and the weather clear, the storm was encountered with better spirits than that in the *Bay of Biscay*. The rolling of our ship occasioned one man to break his leg, and a second his collar bone. The next morning we were but four sail in company, but we rejoined the remainder of the convoy lying to a-head. Running at an averaged rate of six knots, we early on Sunday, the 7th, got sight of *Palmas*, the westernmost of the *Teneriffe* Islands: about noon it was abreast of us, bearing west about three leagues: it was involved in mist, but its summit could be easily discerned towering above the clouds, and covered with snow; the side opposed to us appeared barren, and certainly uninhabited. We hove to during this afternoon, in the course of which the Nereide frigate rejoined us, after several days separation. It had been imagined that she had put back to *England*, but it appeared that having lost sight of us she chased, off *Portugal*, a Spanish corvette and merchantman, both of which she had captured, dismissing the trader, and leaving the corvette to follow her to the place of rendezvous. About five P. M. the signal for bearing away to the southward gave the death blow to the report circulated by the authors of the *Teneriffe* expedition.

Having now entered the trade-wind, which constantly blows in these latitudes between the N. E. and E. points, we calculated pretty certainly on making the *Cape de Verd Islands* in eight days. Nothing occurred to relieve the tediousness of the voyage until the 10th, when we crossed the Tropic of Cancer. The old seamen on board did not let slip this opportunity of levying, in the name of the monarch of the ocean, the usual tribute from those who had never before entered the precincts of his court. Such persons, as from the plea of poverty, or the denial of his authority, refused to comply with the demand, gave Neptune's deputies the peculiar enjoyment of shaving these refractory gentlemen *à la marine,* a description of which ceremony may perhaps not prove unentertaining.

The chief actors in this farce, Neptune, Amphitrite, and a principal attendant as barber, personified by seamen, having painted their faces and dressed themselves in proper costume, with old sacks, powdered wigs made of oakum, and indeed with every article a seaman's fancy could think of as grotesque, the subjects for the razor were ordered between decks, several tubs were then placed round the capstan, and filled with salt water. The watery god and suite having privately reached the ship's bow, hailed her from thence through a speaking trumpet, enquiring her name, that of her commander, her destination, &c. &c. Having received the proper answers, he ordered us to heave to and throw ropes out to himself and company, as he felt inclined to visit the crew. They were drawn on a grating to the capstan, Neptune, properly armed with a set of grains for a trident, and his chief attendant bearing in his hand a rusty piece of hoop and a tar-keg, as the implements of his office: it would have been impossible for any one to have preserved his gravity at the sight of these personages. After the usual greetings, and his congratulations at our safe arrival into his dominions, the sea monarch's queen observed to him that there appeared many strange faces on board; at least she did not recollect ever having observed them in that neighbourhood before: having pointed them out, and, upon examination, finding them strangers to a tropical climate, he made the usual demand of a half gallon of run from each, which was immediately granted by all the officers on board but three, who had paid it on former occasions. Those who were to come under the hands of the barber were now demanded from the master of the ship, and the first subject was brought up blindfold. Being seated on a bar placed across one of the tubs, various questions were put to him by the operators, and an oath administered of much the same nature as that at the Horns at *Highgate;* it was sealed by a kiss imprinted on the carpenter's axe smeared over with a preparation of tar and other ingredients, possessing by no means the most savoury or odoriferous qualities. The like composition having been rubbed over the victim's face, the hacked substitute for a razor was drawn over it, to the no small torture of the patient, and entertainment of the performers and spectators: the bar being suddenly jerked away, he was soused over head and ears in the tub, out of which he was not allowed to escape without a good ducking. The same operation was undergone by all those in waiting, and with very good humour, one seaman alone excepted: this man was a Russian, and became sulky on the occasion, for which he paid very dearly, as he was handled so roughly during the ceremony, that he was forced to call out repeatedly for mercy frem his tormentors. The whole ended as might naturally be supposed, in a drunken frolic, at the expence of many a black eye and bloody nose. It would be unjust not to notice the admirable humour with which the three chief parts of this farce were supported: the man who was the Amphitrite of the day was not even recognized by his own comrades.

CHAPTER III.

Arrival at St. Jago.—*Occurrences there, and Departure.*

WE continued on the same point of the compass with a fine breeze at east, running at six knots, and sometimes eight, until Friday the 12th, when we steered S.S.W. and afterwards S. by W. We were highly delighted on the preceding evening, with the beautiful appearance presented by the new moon: that part of her orb not immediately illuminated by the sun, received a strong light reflected from the earth, a phœnomenon rather new to those on board our vessel. The frigate was dispatched this afternoon under a press of canvas, supposed to make land, and the convoy shortened sail for the night. About ten in the morning of the 13th, we got sight of a high cone, bearing W. by N. From our courses and distances on the chart, we concluded it to be the *Isle of Salt,* the northernmost of the *Cape de Verds,* and its bearings compared with our latitude by observation, confirmed us in this opinion; but we afterwards found we were in error, as this island proved to be *Bonavista*, much to the southward of *Salt Island*. The chart is certainly incorrect as to the position of these two islands. In the afternoon, the Commodore made the signal to prepare to anchor, which we did (after passing close to the *Isle of Mayo*) the next morning at eleven, in *Porto Praya*, on the southern side of *St. Jago*, the largest of the *Cape de Verd Islands*.

Some intercourse having taken place between the Commodore and the Governor, the place was saluted by the former with thirteen guns, and the compliment returned with the like number. Orders were given to the transports to have no communication with the shore until arrangements should have been completed for establishing a market, and regulating the prices of the different articles. For this purpose the General landed, and was received on shore with a salute of twenty-two guns, which were again repeated on his leaving it. The restriction was then taken off, and the landing-place soon became crowded with boats from the fleet.

All the butchers, who could be supplied from the transports, were immediately employed in slaughtering cattle for the use of the troops, who were to be supplied with fresh meat four days in the week: it was of a very wretched quality. The market-place afforded abundant supplies of goats, turkies, fowls, and all those fruits peculiar to a tropical climate: of European vegetables some long leaved cabbage and lettuce could alone be obtained. The poultry and fruit were obtained at two-thirds of the regulated price, which circumstance can only be attributed to the natives not having yet been made acquainted with them, as they afterwards enhanced the value of their produce, which, by the time we left the island, was nearly trebled. We paid, at first, from four to six pistorines for turkies (five pistorines go to a dollar), one hundred and twenty oranges were given for a dollar, and three cocoa nuts for a pistorine.

Two or three days after our arrival, the fleet commenced watering in regimental divisions. The casks were landed under the east part of the town, at a sandy beach: thence they were rolled into the valley about a half mile, where they were filled from a well, out of which the water was raised by two ships' pumps into a trough, whence four hose led it to as many casks. Eighty hogsheads were thus filled a day, and without making any sensible impression on the well: this surprised us not a little, as we had been led to expect, on the report of such persons as had formerly been here, that we should find much difficulty in watering the fleet in the neighbourhood of the port.

Parties were likewise employed under the direction of the engineers and artillery officers, in establishing batteries on the eastern extremity of the harbour, and others to the westward of the town, with a view of securing the convoy against an attack by sea, as it had been rumoured and credited on our leaving *England*, that several squadrons had sailed from French ports. Instructions were given to commanding officers of regiments to land in such a juncture, and an order of defence given them. The batteries were supplied with cannon from the men of war and transports. Two captains' guards were mounted on shore: they served to assist the police of the island in preserving order among our people on shore: they likewise were instructed to seize all boats belonging to the expedition which should be found at the beach, after sun-set.

About the 20th we began to entertain some apprehensions respecting the vessels we had sent into *Madeira*, on the 4th inst. They however made their appearance on the 23d, and brought us cargoes of no inconsiderable value to the inhabitants of transports, namely, of good Madeira, and at a cheap rate compared with the English prices. It cost us 45l. per pipe, and was issued in the proportion of three gallons to every officer.

In the afternoon of the 28th an alarm was spread through the fleet, in consequence of the naval officer at the telegraph on shore making a report to the Commodore of his having heard a cannonade to windward. The frigate and a schooner were immediately ordered out to reconnoitre, the line-of-battle ships got springs on their cables, commanding officers were summoned before the General, and every arrangement made for immediate defence. We however remained undisturbed for the night; and the return of the frigate and schooner (the latter on the 30th) quieted our alarms, as they could make no discovery of any sail to some distance from the island. When it is said that " our alarms were quieted," it is not to be understood that any arose in respect to personal security, but apprehensions were entertained regarding the expedition, which might be seriously affected by the losses we should probably encounter in men and ships in case of such an attack : our position was such as to enable us to give a good account of a force of much greater superiority. We afterwards learnt that the firing proceeded from some rejoicings at the Island of *Bonavista*.

The 5th and 36th Infantry landed for exercise on the 31st, and reimbarked again in the afternoon. The former were again landed for the General's inspection, the next morning. It is not easy to express sufficiently, the astonishment excited by the appearance and regularity of movements exhibited by a British regiment before the inhabitants of *Porto Praya*, who had been accustomed to view only a ragged and undisciplined assemblage of men armed with useless weapons, and in the character of soldiers. Shops, houses, even the public market was deserted on the occasion; nor did the proprietors think of the risk they run of paying for their curiosity at the price of their merchandize.

It had been intended to land all the troops in turn; but after four regiments had taken this duty, it was discontinued, as preparations were making for quitting the place. On Saturday, the signal was made to unmoor, which occasioned no small bustle, as many ships had not yet provided live stock and other necessaries for a continuation of the voyage, as it had not been expected to continue it previous to the arrival of Admiral Murray, who, it was always supposed, was to join us at this port. Parties were immediately sent to scour the country, but they returned with few supplies, and at a very extravagant rate. The next day, however, the signal for sailing was annulled, and this was reported to have proceeded from the determination of a council of war, to remain one week longer for Admiral Murray, and then sail at all events. As Commodore Stopford's and General Craufurd's instructions were never communicated to the world, it is impossible to reason upon the propriety of a measure, which it appears was contrary to expectations both in *England* and in *South America.*

On the 5th of January the Nereide took her prize out to sea and disposed of her, which she could not well do in port, consistently with the laws of neutrality: her cargo had, nevertheless, been purchased before, by the Commissary-general and others of the fleet, as it consisted of flour and other articles of provisions. The frigate returned in the evening, and the next afternoon hoisted the convoy signal for *Buenos Ayres,* for which place she immediately got under weigh. She was accompanied by eight sail, consisting of five transports with the 9th Light Dragoons on board, and three merchantmen : they shaped their course to the southward.

The General, about this time, assembled the officers commanding ships, on board the head-quarters of their respective corps, and consulted with them about any additional comforts that could be procured for the troops. New scuttles were cut in the decks, to give a more thorough ventilation in the ships; the windsails were enlarged, and every precaution recommended and adopted to secure the health of the troops during a *long voyage*. Cleanliness between decks, and likewise in the persons of the men, were consi-dered as the chief means to guard against disease. Journals of the proceedings on board each ship were ordered to be kept, in which were to be noted the daily consumption of water, the fumi-gation of the ship, cleaning of her bows, the dinner hour of the men, the washing of shirts (which was ordered twice a week), airing of bedding, and in short every circumstance that could be considered of a military nature. Every man, but such as were excepted by the medical gentlemen, was obliged to receive over him, every morning, several pails full of water in the presence of the officer of the day. From seven to ten o'clock in the morning, and from three in the afternoon till sun-set, all persons were to keep the deck. These various precautions were communicated in general orders; and the General, in strictly enforcing the obedience of them, observed that he should certainly recommend strongly to the notice of His Royal Highness the Commander in Chief, such officers commanding troops on board ship as should appear zealous in a duty so materially affecting the expedition, as well as report the neglect of those who should appear guilty of any.

About nine in the morning of Sunday, the 11th of January, the sound of cannon from the men of war attracted our attention, and we had the satisfaction of seeing the top-sails loosened, and the signal for sailing run up to the mast-head. Four weeks had now elapsed since we had entered the harbour; and the two last were spent with much impatience in a place no longer supplying the necessary refreshments, and which could no otherwise make any amends for delay. About noon, the guns were reimbarked from the batteries, the hospital-tents on *Green Island* struck, and the sick removed to the Bellona transport, which had been converted into an hospital-ship: these sick were only a few bad opthalmia cases, and one or two of dysentery; for the fleet was in a most healthy state. At

E

three in the afternoon, the convoy began to weigh, and by the time it became dark, the whole were out. We lay to for the night, drifting to the southward ; and at day-light the next morning steered the same course by signal, with a fine breeze at north-east. The Captain and Ganges, seventy-four gun ships, parted from us and stood to the N. W. on their voyage home: the two schooners remained in harbour, and the other men of war accompanied us. We also left at anchor, an American schooner, a Portuguese, and a small French vessel. This latter had entered the port on the same day with ourselves: she had on board a cargo of slaves from *Senegal*, and was bound to *Martinique*. The wretched state of forty-two men, women, and children (the former in chains) cooped up in a leaky schooner of not above thirty-five tons burthen, may be better conceived than described. The advocates for this horrid traffic should themselves be obliged to undergo the sufferings of these unhappy victims before any credit should be given to their assertions, " that slaves derive great benefits by becoming such." The neutrality of the port prevented our taking possession of the vessel ; but she was not allowed to quit it ; and the schooners had orders to watch her closely.

CHAPTER IV.

Description of Porto Praya, *with some Account of its Inhabitants.*

S<small>T.</small> *Jago* is the largest of the *Cape de Verd Islands*, of a triangular shape, and to the south-west of the groupe. It is mountainous, and no part of it fertile but the vallies, which consequently are the only inhabited parts : it is healthy at all seasons, excepting during the months of September, October, and part of November, when the rains having set in, fevers arise, which are attended with most dangerous effects. The productions of these islands are the same as are met with in other tropical countries, such as cocoa-nuts, guavas, bananas, oranges, citrons, limes, the cassada root, sugar-cane, and a few pines : the tamarind and plantain trees grow to a very luxuriant size: Indian corn is grown in great plenty, and constitutes the chief article of food for the natives, who consume very little meat. The cotton plant is likewise cultivated, and from it are manufactured shawls for the slave market

on the coast of *Senegal.* Cattle and goats abound
in these islands, and some hogs are found in
them: their horses are small and chiefly used for
riding, as the ass is the beast of burthen of
St. Jago; and it certainly attains in this climate
a degree of beauty not to be observed in the
English ass. Poultry of every description is in
great abundance; and the mountains harbour
numerous flocks of Guinea fowl. We killed some
teal and a few quails. Some beautiful small birds
fly about the vallies, and along the coast hover
numbers of the largest description of vultures.
The only quadruped peculiar to the island is the
small green monkey; it is a beautiful species,
cleanly, and easily tamed.

The Ciudad, or *Ribiera Grande,* situated on
the south side of the island, was formerly the
residence of the Governor, and of course the
chief place in it. It contains a large church and
a convent of Franciscans, in which are twenty-
four monks. A castle commands the town, which
some time back contained some good houses,
built of a stone resembling the *Portland* stone;
but castle and town are now in a state of ruin,
and present nothing but the greatest decay.
Scarcely is an European to be seen in either; a
few miserable creatures alone inhabit these

buildings, in which formerly resided some respectable Portuguese families.

Porto Praya is situated about seven miles to the N. E. of the Ciudad, and at the S. E. extremity of the island. It is now the residence of the Governor, and contains a church, excepting which building, it does not possess another above the description of a hut: even the Governor's habitation is but one of a better appearance. These huts are built in widely detached rows; and the market is held in the most spacious of these divisions: it is not very regularly attended, and the remains of a marble monument lie scattered about it. The harbour is very safe; as ships can ride in from six to twelve fathoms, with a fine sandy bottom, and completely sheltered from the N. E. wind, which constantly blows here. There is not the least difficulty in getting in; and ships may put to sea at any time. This harbour is defended by a battery of sixteen guns placed at the bottom of the bay, but such is the state of the carriages on which they are mounted, that they just possess strength enough to bear the shock of firing a salute.

All the other inhabited places of the island are such only, as where the temptation of a good spring of water has brought together some families, who build their huts without any order. It was not possible to obtain any correct information respecting the population of the island, so various were the accounts : it may, however, be rated at twenty thousand, one-half of whom are slaves, obtained from the neighbouring coast. The free inhabitants are either the black descendants of the Aborigines, or a Mulatto race between them and the Portuguese. They are tall and well built, with a fine upright crrriage : the women are, in particular, very fine figures. The dress of the men consists of a white cotton jacket and trowsers; some wear only a shirt and drawers; others the latter only. The women generally wear cotton petticoats reaching to the knees ; a piece of cloth of the same manufacture covers their bodies, and over the whole they have a shawl: this latter article is universally worn by all descriptions of women, free or slaves; and they throw it over their shoulders with a grace peculiar to them-selves: some women were seen with silk bodices. The heads of both sexes are close shaved, round which some wear a handkerchief in form of a turban. The few Portuguese traders in the island dress in the European style.

The only language spoken is Portuguese; and these islands having always been subject to

Portugal, the Roman Catholic religion is alone tolerated in them. Though loaded with scapularies and beads, the inhabitants do not appear to undergo many bodily mortifications. With the exception of the Franciscans at *Ribiera Grande*, the priests are blacks, and ordained in the islands. Confession takes place but once a year, and on Sunday only is mass performed. The guard alone preserve any public shew of religion on week days, by chaunting in line a particular hymn, at noon and at eve. They are not particularly nice in having the attendance of a priest at the funerals of their departed friends, whom they commit to the earth a few hours after death, and in the same clothes in which they died: wood is too scarce to afford coffins.

These people are civil and hospitable: the manner in which they treat their slaves is a sure proof of their humane disposition, and a noble example for European proprietors of human beings in the *West Indies*. We found those who resided in the neighbourhood of the harbour much inclined to take advantage of our necessities, as they, in almost every instance, asked twice the sum they would take for their produce. It must, however, be confessed, that within the island they were found much more honest.

The Governor is always an European, and relieved every three years. It is indeed considered more a duty to hold the government, than accepted through choice, so few are the advantages and honors of such a high office in these islands. His pay is trifling, but he derives some profits from the duties levied upon every article bought or sold in the island, as well as on the imports and exports. These latter consist only of some cottons manufactured for the slave-market. Three Portuguese sloops came in while we lay here, and an American, who was obliged to pay a duty of ten per cent. upon some articles brought for the supply of the island. The Governor appears to rule as much by his own humour, as by any known regulations; he exiles to *Africa* without any form of judicial proceeding, and this of course makes his power much dreaded: it is not to be supposed, however, that he is not amenable to the Court at *Lisbon* for acts of gross oppression and tyranny. The military force of the island consists of two or three companies of regular infantry, and about a thousand militia, cavalry and infantry. The officers alone of the infantry have any thing uniform in dress; the men are in ragged shirts and trowsers, and armed with broken firelocks, and other military appointments in equal condition : they are as badly paid as clothed. The mounted militia are dressed in blue ; but as they are obliged to perform service one fort'night in six weeks, for about sixpence per day, it is not to be imagined they can make such an appearance as our English cavalry : it is well in a *St. Jago* troop of horse to find twenty pairs of breeches and boots.

While at *Porto Praya* we observed, with the greatest effect, that beautiful appearance which is presented at night by the tropical seas, when agitated. On our passage, the sparks emitted at the bows of the ship, and the stream of light under her stern, excited in no small degree our admiration ; but it was reserved for this harbour to give us a spectacle, which required no very poetical fancy to raise it into the effect of enchantment. In the calm of night, the boats plying about the fleet could only be discovered approaching by the body of animated fire surrounding them : they appeared like those monsters of romance, breathing flames, with wings of fire, and followed by a train of the same elemental fluid. We no where else during our long voyage witnessed these effects to a similar degree, and we attributed them at *Porto Praya* to the great quantity of phosphoric matter impregnating the

F

water of the harbour. The fish in it were so numerous as to occasion every morning an agitation
about the ships, equal to what would be excited
by a fresh breeze. We frequently caught above
five hundred weight of large mullet at one draught
of the net. The inhabitants are too indolent to
take advantage of such a supply, which could
easily be obtained by fishing from the rocks, for
they have no boats.

CHAPTER V.

Passage to the Cape of Good Hope.—*Occurrences there, and Departure for* St. Helena.

On leaving *St. Jago* we were in the same state of uncertainty respecting the object of the expedition as we had been at our arrival. The Spanish possessions in the *Gulph of Mexico* were considered by most persons in the fleet as likely to become the theatre of our military operations. By the accounts of such mariners as had doubled *Cape Horn,* it appeared impossible for us to arrive there in the season most favorable for such a passage, particularly with so large a fleet; and it would also be necessary for us to lose more time at some other intermediate port, to obtain supplies we could not dispense with. As to any operations in the eastern seas, no person had ever given them a thought. A very short period of time soon put an end to our prospects in *North America;* for, not altering our course to the westward in twenty-four hours after sailing, our views became directed elsewhere, and we looked forward to touching at the *Brazils* for fuel, &c.

We were carried along to the southward, by the N. E. trade-wind, until the 15th, when we were in lat. 8° 50′ N. and began to experience the variation of the winds; they soon settled again in the N. E. and run us by the 17th as far as 3° 57′ N. where we fell in with the calms which are prevalent about the Equator. A very heavy thunder storm came on during the night; one of the thunderbolts struck the rigging of the Waare store-ship, and carried away her main-top mast, and shivered the main mast: for several days previous to this we had met with heavy showers. On the 18th, finding the Campion to be so dull a sailer as to occasion much delay to the convoy, the Commodore had the stores and troops removed from her into other vessels, and ordered her to make the appointed rendezvous as well as she could: we lost sight of her about the beginning of the ensuing month.

It was not before the 29th of January that we crossed the Equator, which we did in 22° of west longitude. During this time nothing worth recording took place, excepting our falling in with a ship and brig on the 25th, which were chaced by the Commodore: the ship was alone reached, and proved to be an American bound to the *East Indies;* she was permitted to continue her course.

The sharks were daily gathered about us; but as we had very bad fishing tackle, we only succeeded in catching one about four feet and a half in length. Owing to the same cause, we caught but few bonettas, which were in extensive shoals, as well as the albacores. They played about at times in such numbers as to occasion the appearance of the sea breaking over a reef in a fresh breeze, and accompanied with a like noise: we felt inclined from this circumstance to account for a shoal being marked down in Heather's chart, in latitude 2° 08′ N. and longitude 22° 15′ W. called *Cæsar's Breakers,* upon which spot we actually were on the 23d of this month, and must have noticed them, if any such had existed.

On the 1st of February, when we had passed the line about two degrees, the wind appeared to settle in the S. E. between which and the E. point it blew until the 16th, by which time we had reached 23° 22′ S. The signal having been made to steer S. E. no doubts remained respecting our touching at the *Cape of Good Hope.* A hint of this nature had already spread through the fleet, upon the authority of some officers, who, having obtained possession of a copy of the Naval Code of Signals, had observed a communication to this effect between the men of war. These officers were obliged to surrender them, upon the requisition of the Commodore, enforced by the authority of the General. A report to the like effect had also got into the fleet from a bark which passed through us on the 2d of February, after thirty-four days passage from *England:* she was bound for *Buenos Ayres.* We learnt from her that our expected convoy was to join us at the *Cape of Good Hope.* She gave us some papers, and we were gratified at obtaining some European intelligence, the first since we had left that quarter of the globe.

Finding that we were not to put into any port along the Brazil coast, and that four or five weeks were likely to elapse before making the *Cape,* we began seriously to take into consideration the state of our stock of fresh provisions, which, having been laid in for a much shorter voyage, now bore but a small proportion to what was necessary for our daily consumption. Three goats (nearly starved), two pigs, and about half a dozen turkies, composed all our stock. We had, to be sure, a cow on board; but she supplied us with milk for our breakfast, and we were therefore very loth to give her over to the butcher, particularly as she was not much in flesh, having long before this consumed what grass we had laid in at *St. Jago ;* and her appetite was not sufficiently strong to relish our substitutes. Of vegetables we had no more. We became obliged to reduce our fresh stock to as small a daily consumption as possible ; and we even allotted two days in the week to be without, when the ship's rations alone composed our meals. The like economy was established with respect to our wine, of which, having been at first too profuse, we now felt very deficient.

Symptoms of dysentery now appeared in some ships: two men afflicted with it were removed from ours to the Bellona, on board of which five persons had died since leaving *St. Jago ;* two of fever, and three of dysentery. An officer of the 88th, and an hospital mate, had also been carried off by fevers. Several of the gentlemen of our ship were disordered in the bowels, but through the attention of the Surgeon on board, who took all the pains imaginable to check the complaint in its dawn, they soon recovered. In other respects, if a few slight opthalmia cases be excepted, the ship was in a very healthy state.

We obtained several flying-fish, which being

chased by the albacores and bonettas fell on the deck. They rose in swarms out of the water, and were of various dimensions, but in general about the size of a herring, and bearing in form a strong resemblance to this fish. At a very little distance behind the head were placed the fins, by which it suspended itself out of the water: when in it they lay close to the body, and extended nearly to the tail; they opened out like a fan. It was not one single exertion which raised the fish above the water, but a real flight performed by the action of the wings, and which was at times above two hundred yards in length, and in evolutions.

In the afternoon of the 13th we stood by signal to the northward. The Commodore was apprehensive of running during the night on the *Isle of Trinidada*, which was, however, far to the westward of us. We continued our course again about midnight. On the 16th we were in long. 27° 49′ W. and lat. 23° 22′ S. when the wind began to vary; accordingly the signal was made for us to steer S. E. Two strange sail appeared on the 17th, but they were not spoken. From the 19th to the 22d we experienced very tempestuous weather from the southward: the rain at times fell in perfect torrents.

·On the 24th we were not a little surprised at seeing the Campion coming down upon us from the westward: she had parted on the 2d, owing to her dull sailing. Having stood more to the westward than the fleet, she had fallen in much earlier with the westerly winds. She soon dropped a-stern again; but having the advantages which generally attend a single ship, she made the *Cape* five days before us.

We now had the wind from the N.N.W. with but little variation, until the 5th of March, when it blew from the southward: but it again, the next morning, settled in the old quarter. On this day, at noon, we had run as far to the eastward as in 1° 02′ east longitude, and in latitude 33° 54′, when the Haughty gun-brig crowded sail, and stood from the fleet for the *Cape of Good Hope.* The weather, during the whole of this time, was remarkably fair, and the sea perfectly smooth, though at times we ran at the rate of nine knots.

From the 9th to the 16th, we were obliged to beat up towards the *Cape,* as the winds were now prevalent from the southward and eastward. We stood our course on the 17th, and were in expectation of making land in the evening; but as the wind failed us, we were disappointed. The

G

Theseus, 74, stood in towards *Table Bay*; and the next morning we had the satisfaction of beholding the high land of the southern extremity of *Africa*, extending from the *Table Mountain* to the *Cape of Good Hope*, and some hours after the mountainous parts of *Hottentot Holland* rose to our view, in detached hillocks. From our course it evidently appeared to be the Commodore's intention to put into *False Bay*, a circumstance not very agreeable to those of the expedition, as this bay was said, by such as had frequented the *Cape*, to be by no means capable of supplying our wants; these will be supposed to have been far from trifling, when it is mentioned, that in our vessel, we had been living for weeks past entirely on the ship's provisions, and that our wine had been out above three: few ships of the fleet were better circumstanced. Besides this consideration, many of the officers embarked had acquaintances among the troops serving at the *Cape*, and few were on duty at *Simon's Town*, the only quarter in this bay, and which is removed above twenty-five miles from *Cape Town*. At noon we had passed the *Bellows Breakers*, which lie about one mile off the *Cape*; the wind blowing directly down the bay, the convoy were obliged to beat up, and continued doing so until about midnight, although the Commodore had made the signal to anchor *immediately;* but not setting the example, it was not attended to. The next morning early, the whole fleet anchored about four or five hundred yards from *Simon's Town,* called after the little bay in which it is situated.

Boats immediately put off for the shore, in hopes of obtaining supplies of fresh meat and wine; of the former none could be procured, as no preparations had been made for our reception at this place: our arrival having been expected at *Table Bay,* cattle had been driven there for our use, and supplies of vegetables conveyed. Our vexation may be much better conceived than expressed, and the motives for taking us into a port, bare of every indispensable supply, when a much nearer one could yield us every comfort, were not a little commented upon. Admiral Murray, with two 64-gun ships, and some smaller armed vessels, had arrived, a few days before, in *Table Bay,* where he expected to have found us ready to put to sea immediately: he did not conceal his chagrin at our having been taken into *False Bay,* and immediately sent an order to our Commodore, to take us round, without loss of time, to *Table Bay.* In compliance with this order, we weighed on Sunday the 22d, and stood out to sea, to the westward, until midnight, when the fleet tacked, and made for *Table Bay*. When under the *Lion's Head*, several of the vessels became suddenly becalmed, although others not above one hundred yards from them continued standing into the bay at the rate of four knots. The becalmed ships drifted fast towards some rocks near *Camp's Bay*, and were obliged to be towed off, until they got into a current of air. When clear of the *Lion's Rump*, they were as suddenly attacked with a strong gale from the S.E. which carried away various parts of the rigging. Most of the fleet got to the anchoring ground, but others, after beating about for several hours, were obliged to bring up in the middle of the bay: the whole anchored safely the next morning about one mile and a half from the town.

We found at anchor in *Table Bay*, the Polyphemus, sixty-four gun ship, with Rear Admiral Murray's flag, the Africa sixty-four, the Nereide frigate, that had conveyed the Ninth Light Dragoons to *Buenos Ayres*, the Camel naval store-ship, the Fly sloop of war brig that had brought dispatches respecting our expedition, two gun brigs, and a small schooner: these were all the armed vessels. There were several other ships, transports, and merchantmen, but no Indiamen.

The convoy instantly set about watering and taking in provisions, in which they were employed with the utmost expedition, as it was necessary for us to quit this place before the change of the monsoon, when the wind setting violently on the shore, and rolling in a heavy sea, renders it very unsafe to remain at this anchorage: the change was expected to take place about the middle of April. The day after our arrival the sick from the hospital-ship were landed, and provided with accommodations on shore: a convalescent hospital was also established. Fourteen had died on board the hospital-ship during the passage: very few in other vessels. The whole that were landed amounted to about eighty, who soon began to experience the good effects of a change of air and diet.

The Paulina, sloop of war, was dispatched for *England* on the 26th of March, and she was followed on the 29th by the Spencer and Theseus. These were to proceed for *St. Helena*, and wait there some days, in case of the arrival of homeward-bound Indiamen, whom they were to take in charge. Several officers in bad health, and from other causes, obtained leave to go home in them.

A regiment of the expedition was landed daily

for exercise and inspection; this was done by each in turn: they always reimbarked immediately after the inspection. It was particularly gratifying to see these troops, after having been so long embarked, go through their evolutions as if they had been months preparing for a review. In every respect they afforded great satisfaction to General Craufurd: he was, however, under the very unpleasant necessity of ordering a general court martial on some officers, whose conduct on board ship had been such as to oblige their commanders to report them.

Bat and forage for two hundred days, and a month's additional pay in advance, were issued. These sums were soon expended in laying in stock for continuing the voyage, which still remained a profound secret. Strong rumours were afloat respecting the dispatches brought by the Fly brig, which had left *England* two or three days after Admiral Murray: they were said to order us to *Buenos Ayres* to repair the disasters encountered by General Beresford, and to make up the losses Sir Samuel Auchmuty had met with in the assault of *Monte Video*. We had received these details by the Nereide. The recapture of *Buenos Ayres* by the Spaniards was not officially known in *England,* at the departure of Admiral Murray, although a report to this effect had been in circulation since the beginning of November. We laid in four months' stock, and at a very reasonable rate, as sheep and vegetables abounded. Poultry was the only extravagant article of supply, Our live stock and wine stood us in about 20*l.* for each officer.

On Saturday, the 4th of April, an order was issued for all persons belonging to the fleet to be on board their respective ships by three o'clock in the afternoon, at which time parties from every regiment were landed to pick up stragglers, and blue Peter was hoisted on board the men of war. Notwithstanding these early precautions, it was with difficulty the drunken soldiers on shore could be collected together; and the General was obliged to act in person at the pier, to get off the different boats, which was not completely effected before midnight. The next morning, the signal was made to unmoor, and we were expecting that for getting under weigh, but the wind freshening about noon, the ships of war were obliged to strike top-gallant yards and masts. The *Table Hill* now put on the cap foreboding wind, and assumed a threatening aspect: during the afternoon it came on to blow tremendously from the south-east: the wind raised a spray from the surface of the water, which, mixed with the sand from the beach, prevented our seeing the town, although the sky was perfectly serene over-head. The Admiral drove in the evening, and lost two anchors in attempting to bring up: he was obliged to keep beating about for the night.

While under some apprehensions from the violent effects of the wind, eight large sail appeared at the back of the *Lion*, and when under his *Rump* were almost becalmed; as soon as they had cleared this they began to feel the wind rushing over the low ground to the eastward of the *Table Mountain*, which obliged them to close reef, and stand under topsails only into the bay. One of them, bearing a pendant, having communicated by telegraph with Admiral Murray, she made the signal to put to sea again, which they immediately did, as it was impossible for them to make the anchoring ground: they were homeward-bound Chinamen, and bore away for *St. Helena.*

General Craufurd having embarked the preceding morning on board the Polyphemus (where he was received with a salute of thirteen guns), the fleet began to get under weigh about ten in the morning of Monday, with a very light breeze from the S.W. We stood out of the bay by the passage east of *Robben Island:* previous to quitting it, the Admiral saluted the castle with thirteen guns, and received the like number in return. There was but little wind during the night, and on the 7th, several sail being missing, we put about in expectation of meeting them; but having made the land by the evening without getting sight of the absentees, we once more stood off to the N. W. with a pleasant breeze from the S.W. The next morning the whole convoy joined, and we bore away to the N. N.W. with the wind directly aft, and carrying us at the rate of five knots.

Having nothing of greater moment to engage our attention at present, a brief account of the *Cape* settlement may not prove uninteresting.

CHAPTER VI.

Some Account of the Cape *Settlement.*

C_{APE} *Town* is situated at the bottom of *Table Bay,* which takes its name from the high land rising immediately from it, and presenting to the spectator at sea, a flat extending about one and a half mile east and west. This town is regularly laid out in rectangular streets, which are spacious and clean. The houses being painted of light colours on the outside, wear a light and neat appearance; they are built of stone or brick, and have their fronts embellished with some pieces of statuary or ornamental architecture: the rooms are spacious and lofty; and, to keep them cool, floored with tile: there is rarely above one apartment comfortably furnished. There are three public squares, one of which contains the Stadthouse, situated nearly in the centre of the town: the easternmost square contains a church, whose roof is supported within by four large plain columns; it is not adorned with any embellishments, but has nearly the whole of the interior surface covered with clumsy monuments and escutcheons: here the troops of the garrison assemble at divine service. Another church is placed at the west end of the town, and frequented by Calvinists. There is but one inn (the British Hotel) in the place; but no genteel stranger need feel at a loss for accommodations, as the best families in the place will receive him as a boarder and lodger on moderate terms.

The *Government Gardens*, formerly belonging to the Dutch Company, are at the back of the town, and leading immediately from the *Church Square.* They are spacious and well-planted, affording a pleasing shelter from the noon heat of this climate, and they are at all times accessible to decent persons. On the Sunday evenings they are crowded with the ladies attracted hither by the music of the regimental bands which attend on these occasions. The Governor's residence is placed in these grounds; and at the upper end is an ornamental colonnade conducting to a row of dens for the reception of curious beasts. At the time of our arrival, these consisted only of a pair of lions, who had, besides, an extensive walk enclosed with a strong wall about twelve feet high, with openings well secured with iron bars; these animals were not above two years old, and had been reared by the woman who had charge of the buildings. A little anecdote respecting them, and related by the keeper, deserves to be recorded: it occurred but a short time previous to our arrival, and will tend to confirm the opinion maintained by most naturalists, of the lion being in possession of more noble qualities than are found in other carnivorous animals, or indeed in any other of the brute creation.

Several gentlemen brought to these dens two dogs, to enjoy the very peculiar gratification of seeing them devoured by the lions: one of them being thrown into the area soon fell a victim to their appetites: the second, in tumbling from the wall surrounding the area, broke his leg, and howled most bitterly at the pain it occasioned him. The lions approached to sacrifice him as they had done the first; but in drawing near, the male appearing to commisserate the unhappy situation of the little victim, stopped short, and prevented his spouse from attacking it. She appearing determined to carry her point, a violent struggle ensued between the royal pair, and he at last succeeded in keeping her off, himself doing the office of safeguard to the poor dog. The gentlemen who had come with such humane motives of entertainment, took the lesson taught

them by the noble brute, and employed the keeper
to extricate the dog: he coaxed the lions into
their dens, and entering the area released the
little wretch, whom he now shews as no common
object of curiosity. In telling this little story, it
is not meant to convey the idea that ladies are
always more ferocious than the other sex: and it
will be but doing justice to the above queen of
beasts to add, that she had been lately deprived
of her young, which circumstance may in some
degree account for her additional ferocity.

To the eastward of the town, and across the
Grand Parade, a remarkably fine one, is situated
the castle: it is a regular pentagon, said to have
been constructed by the famous Coehorn, on his
way to *India*. Round the counterscarp is raised
a second parapet, fronted by another ditch, which
is again defended by a covered way to the eastward. This second parapet is partly washed at
high water by the sea, and mounted, in this direction, with very heavy guns and mortars; among
them are some beautiful brass pieces. There is
but one entrance into the body of the place, and
it is on the town side; but there is a passage
through the counterguard leading into the
country; both are defended with ravelins, that
in front of the eastern passage having retired

flanks. The whole of the works are rivetted with stone. In the castle are the commandant's quarters, and it contained at this time three companies of the Royal Artillery, and the 24th Infantry. The other troops of the garrison, consisting of the 21st Light Dragoons, 4th battalion 60th, 72d, and 93d Regiments, were in barracks about four hundred yards behind the castle; buildings originally intended as warehouses for the Dutch Company, and which, although in an unfinished state, were superior accommodations for troops. From the castle runs an intrenchment along the beach, flanked at certain distances with artillery: at the distance of about one thousand yards it takes a rectangular direction, and ascends for about seven hundred yards: this last face is defended by four small redoubts, and the only parts of the lines that are kept in any state of repair, the intermediate spaces being entirely in ruins. A heavy battery covering a strong tower, called after General Craig, is placed about a half mile in advance of the lines: two block-houses, about one mile asunder, stand nearly at the foot of the perpendicular rock above them. An enemy in possession of these two buildings would render the whole of the works already described perfectly useless. To the north-west of the town, and at the bottom of the *Lion's Rump*, are three very heavy enclosed batteries, which command the entrance of the bay in this direction, as well as a great part of it after ships have entered: in that called the *Amsterdam*, and the nearest to the town, are confined the prisoners of war, and the convicts condemned to labour on the public works. These batteries appear to have been more judiciously constructed for securing the town against a naval attack, than are the lines calculated to prevent a force, after effecting a landing to the eastward, from entering it.

Ships moor abreast of the town, the largest about one mile east of *Amsterdam Battery*, and smaller vessels about half that distance from the shore: the bottom is sandy. This anchorage is always used during the S. E. monsoon, which prevails from the middle of August to much the same time in April, when the wind setting in from the N. W. brings along with it the whole *Atlantic*, and renders it so unsafe for ships, that the underwriters are not considered liable for vessels remaining in *Table Bay* after the 14th of April: this sea is very little broken by a low sandy island, called *Robben Island*, about five miles from either side of the bay. It often happens that vessels are driven from their anchors by the violent gusts which rush down from *Table Mountain ;* but as it always gives notice of these passionate fits, by collecting the white clouds about its summit, few are taken unprepared, and if forced from their anchors can very easily put to sea. The only landing-place is at a wooden pier under the castle: on each side of it run conductors, with cocks to them, at which boats water with the greatest facility; eight may do it at the same time. It is curious to see the black boys collected about this pier fishing for herring, which they catch by means of four hooks fastened together at the end of a piece of twine, about four yards long: they throw them into the water, and are always sure of hooking a fish in some part of the body, once in three or four throws.

The markets afford the greatest plenty of meat and vegetables. The beef is not very good, owing to the scarcity of grass, which is, besides, rank and sour. The ox, though equally large with the English, wants that richness of feeding which renders our meat so superior to that of every other country: he appears to be bred at the *Cape* more for purposes of draught than to supply the necessities of the table.

. If the beef is not very good, the mutton of the

country makes sufficient amends: it is pretty well fattened, and has a delicate flavour. The *Cape* sheep are bred in great numbers, and are well known by the peculiar formation of the tail: this is a solid lump of fat, about eight inches wide at the insertion, and decreasing to a point, curling upward. This fat, about seven or eight pounds in weight, is substituted for butter in culinary uses, and serves when dried, as portable food, with a little bread and salt, for the slaves who perform their labours at a distance from home. Poultry is very extravagant. Numbers of young ostriches were driven in by the natives to be disposed of to such collectors of natural curiosities as could afford to give two or three guineas a pair for these birds. A young lion was purchased in the market for about seven guineas.

The fertile parts of the country produce plenty of corn; and it seldom happens that an importation of this grain is necessary: the bread of the *Cape* is good. The only good wines cultivated are white, excepting the red Constantia, which, however, does not bear any proportion in quantity to the others. The best *Cape* Madeira may be had for about *5s.* per gallon: the smaller wines are very cheap, but not a safe beverage.

The inhabitants of *Cape Town*, of European

I

descent are Dutch, with very few exceptions;
and the Dutch manners are prevalent. The
phlegmatic disposition of the Hollanders seems
to have encreased upon their African brethren,
both from the nature of the climate, and the
indolence which prevails among them, as every
domestic and handicraft office is performed by
their numerous slaves. The labour of these
slaves composes almost the whole revenue of their
proprietors: they are taught every trade, and let
out by the day as horses and cattle are in *Europe*.
The males are not treated with the greatest
humanity; but the females are particularly in-
dulged, for the sake of the children they bear; so
highly valued in this settlement is the traffic in
human flesh. Slaves bore a very high price at our
arrival, owing to a great mortality occasioned by
the introduction of the meazles in a cargo from
Mozambique. The white children had suffered
but little less, and in two months above seven
hundred of them were carried off by a disorder
which could not but prove fatal among a people
so little prepared for the infection: about eight
hundred slaves fell victims to it, and it had nearly
disappeared when we left the *Cape*.

The *Cape* women in their youth have pleasing
countenances, and most beautiful forms: they

soon, however, grow fat, and shew in person as well as language that they are closely allied to the Hollanders. They love dress, and exhibit much taste in their attire, which is after the European fashion. It were desirable to be enabled to say as much of the morals of the young ladies of the *Cape*, as of their persons, but the information collected from those gentlemen who had resided some time among them, was not very favorable in this respect.

The population of the town in whites may be about seven thousand, and the number of slaves nearly double. These are kept in a proper state of discipline by a strong and watchful police. In every street, and at every hour of the day, peace officers armed with swords are to be met with, who take immediate cognizance of disorders arising among the Malays; and it is remarked, that the most dreaded of these officers are such of their own people as have obtained emancipation: a few Hottentots are likewise employed in the inferior police offices, and found useful and trust-worthy. A slave cannot make his appearance in the streets at night without a lighted lanthorn, or he is committed to prison. Notwithstanding all these precautions, the Malay disposition breaks out at times, and renders capital punishments frequent in this colony. It must however be observed, that in addition to the heavy misfortune of being in a state of bondage, the unhappy slaves at the *Cape* have that of being the property of masters who possess but few, if any, of those qualities of the heart which tend towards regulating the conduct of superiors in favor of their inferiors, by which inferiority becomes a much lighter weight, than when it is constantly felt from the exertion of an oppressive and tyrannical authority.

We saw but very few of the Aborigines in their native dress, and none ornamented in the style represented by those who have given the public an account of their travels in the interior. Such Hottentots as presented themselves to our view, certainly appeared to have been but little favored by nature in their persons. The Esquimaux of Labrador are, to be sure, mean in the scale of human creation, but they bear the palm from their fellow creatures at the southern extremity of *Africa.* It is not to be doubted but that the SUPREME BEING has given life to this humble race, to fulfil some of the purposes for which, in his wisdom, he has created all things; but it is hoped that it will not be deemed impious or uncharitable to say, that this degenerate branch of the human species, seems only fitted to enter upon the humblest offices assigned to man. The writer of this narrative would have acted an illiberal part to have established this opinion on his own observations, as he had not time or opportunity of forming any, but from all the information obtained from those strangers who had resided much here, these ideas were the result. It is very probable that under any other governors but the Dutch, the Hottentots might, ere this, have appeared to greater advantage; and every well wisher to the human race will join their wishes that this may be the case on a future day.

The territory depending on the *Cape* government is divided into six districts; at the head of each presides a landrost. The officer commanding at *Algoa Bay*, about three hundred miles east of *Cape Town*, acts as landrost over the district of *Uitenhage;* and this command is considered as a post of much emolument, as well as authority. A natural hot-bath about one hundred miles in the interior is under the direction of government: it is much resorted to by invalids, and said to be productive of excellent effects.

The inhabitants were left, after the surrender of the settlement, in full possession of the form of government then existing; subject, however, to the superintendance of a governor appointed from *England.* The chief civil administration is vested in the hands of the Fiscal, and the officers under the old government. The execution by breaking on the wheel has been abolished by us in criminal cases, for which hanging has been substituted. This last mode of punishment is said not to produce so efficient a check on the Malays as the old one, from the superstitious idea, inculcated by their religion, that they cannot enter into the habitations of the blessed after death, with muti-lated limbs. Condemnation to labour in chains for life, or a term of years, on the public works, is the punishment for offences not incurring death. The police of the *Cape* is said to be the best regulated out of *Europe.* A gazette is published weekly, under the inspection of the Governor; it chiefly contains proclamations and advertisements in Dutch and English: the means of circulating it are by a post waggon, which leaves town on Mondays and Fridays; and by post-office runners, who, on foot, convey letters to many parts of the country with much celerity.

For a twelvemonth previous to our taking possession of the *Cape,* it was perfectly destitute of every article of European manufacture; so

much so, that even the best description of inhabitants had barely decent covering for their
persons. As they have no produce, but for their
own consumption, and no manufactories, nearly
the whole of the returns they make for European
goods is in bullion, which renders it so valuable,
that the soldier who receives his pay in dollars at
4s. 8d. each, disposes of them again for 6s. 5d. in
the paper currency, the only circulating medium
of the country. Bills on *England* bear an equal
premium: these fell, however, during our stay, as
we brought a greater amount into the market
than there was immediately a demand for. It was
said that, at the capture, Spanish dollars sold
at 12s.

CHAPTER VII.

Continuation of the Description.

THE great object of curiosity to a stranger arriving at the *Cape* is *Table Mountain,* one ascent to which is generally considered by all those who have made it, as amply sufficient, such is the fatigue encountered in this short journey. A party was made for this undertaking on the morning of the 2d of April. We started at half an hour after four, in order to have the benefit of the moon to lead us to the foot of the perpendicular face of the hill, and to avoid, as much as possible, the heat of the sun. The sky was very serene, and a heavy dew falling. We followed the direction of a small rivulet, and about one mile from the town arrived at a water-mill, where we stopped for some time to view a fire that had broken out in the middle of the town, and which presented a beautiful appearance from this spot, whence we completely overlooked the whole of the buildings: here the swellings of ground became more sudden. We learnt from the miller, that two adventurers had preceded us about half an hour. At a quarter before six we reached the foot of the steep, which appeared to us to be about one half the height from the level of the sea to the top of the mountain. The stream now divided into several branches, and we followed the principal one. The whole face of the rock now became illuminated by the rising sun, and we beheld, labouring among the rocks about three hundred yards above us, an officer of engineers in full uniform, with sash and sword, accompanied by another person in plain clothes. The heat began to oppress us, and momentary halts were necessary at every ten or twelve paces, as the ascent did not decline above fifteen degrees from the perpendicular, excepting where we were obliged to wind round the foot of some detached rock: we had lost sight of the rivulet for some time. A little after seven, we reached a resting place, where the slaves, who come hither in search of fuel, had scooped a hole in the recess of the rock to receive its drippings: here we overtook the two gentlemen who had preceded us, and to whom we offered the use of our refreshments, as they had not thought of the necessity of providing for the calls of the stomach. In a quarter of an hour, we proceeded on our expedition, which now began to wear the prospect

K

of a termination, and a few minutes before eight
we passed through the chasm which introduced
us to the *Table Land.* This chasm is about twenty
yards wide, the rocks rising on each side like
perpendicular walls: when through it we turned
to the left, and made for the edge of the precipice,
where certainly a very grand spectacle presented
itself to our view from a height of three thousand
six hundred feet. We commanded from this spot
a perfect plan of the harbour and neighbouring
country: the town lay at our feet, and we traced
every part of it without distinguishing the relief
of the buildings. The castle and lines bore the
appearance of models preserved in military col-
lections, and the ships in the bay looked like boats
without masts. At a distance we beheld the mountains over-topping the thick strata of clouds; and
turning round to the south, *False Bay* appeared
close to us. We walked over to the eastern extremity of the flat, and looked down from thence
upon the low land which divides it from the higher
ground of the interior: on this level we descried
some beautiful plantations, interspersed among the
more sandy and dry parts. We could see *False
Cape* very distinctly, and the low inhabited land
of *Hottentot Holland.* The sun now reflected
an excessive heat from the surfaces of the rock,

and we sought shelter from it under the large fragments that are on the top, and where we found an abundant supply of excellent water. We walked over every part of the *Table Land*, and imagined it to be about one mile from the chasm to the eastern extremity; from the same opening to the westward, it may be about half that distance: the broadest part is in the first space, and is five hundred yards, with a gentle declination to the southward. On it are some marshy spots, over-grown with moss and a long dank grass; they are inhabited by frogs, who, with a few birds of a very diminutive size, and some small lizards, were the only living things we met with: the skin of a large snake but lately killed, shewed us, however, that these reptiles are to be found on this inhospitable spot. The large baboon is said to occupy the crevices in the face of the hill, but we did not see the least trace of any. The heath was in beautiful bloom, and a variety of shrubs bore very lively blossoms. At the head of the chasm a valley leads to the right, from the mouth of which *Camp's Bay* is overlooked: this valley being completely sheltered, the shrubbery in it was remarkably rich in leaf and flower. Directly before the chasm is a tremendous precipice, which looks upon all the breaks of the tongue of land extending as far as the *Cape of Good Hope*, properly so called. About noon we entertained some apprehensions of the table cloth spreading, as the clouds were coming from the south-east, and passing over the lower parts of the mountain: our alarm proved false, as the summit kept perfectly clear. About half an hour after two we commenced our descent by the same route which had led us up; and at four we reached the windmill. From this to the town, every part of the stream was occupied with female slaves washing, and the banks were literally covered with linen. It was nearly five when we rested from the fatigues of the day; but which were more than compensated by the sublime prospect which had been laid before us. It may not prove useless to advise such as mean to visit the *Table Land* to start early, to be lightly dressed, and above all to avoid the incumbrances of a *sword and fowling piece*, which can only add to the labour of the bearer, without proving of the least utility or amusement.

In entering the bay by the passage south of *Robben Island*, the town is concealed from view by a curious ridge running north and south, and called the *Lion :* it bears no small resemblance to the figure of this animal in that attitude known in heraldry by the distinctive epithet of *couchant:* this resemblance is almost perfect from the nape of the neck to the tail: the head is formed by a conical rock, the ascent to the top of which is by ropes; on it stands a flag staff, and a second is placed on the *Lion's Rump,* which has been made a signal station. *Camp's Bay* lies at the chest, and as there is a possibility of boats landing in it in very calm weather, and as the distance to a ridge overlooking the town and connecting the *Table Mount* with the *Lion's Head* is not above one mile and a half, it has been made a military post, guarded by an officer and thirty men, who are relieved weekly, and could very easily be reinforced from the garrison in case of necessity. It very seldom happens, however, that the surf is so low as to permit the approach of boats. The green parts about this bay are much frequented by that beautiful bird, called the Sugar Bird; it is various in size and plumage, but resembles much the humming bird of *America:* like this also, it subsists on the juices of flowers, drawn by inserting its long bill: one species has a tail above ten inches in length, to a body not so large as a robin's.

False Bay is to the southward of *Table Bay:* their heads are divided by a low land, about nine or ten miles over. The western side of the first mentioned is formed by the continuation of the chain of rocky hills, of which *Table Mount* is one extreme, and the *Cape of Good Hope* the other: extending about nine leagues. *Hottentot Holland* forms the east side of this harbour, which is a most noble and spacious one, easily entered and sailed from: the anchoring ground is in a small bay, and its position may be immediately distinguished by the white hill which faces the south. In making it, *Roman's Rock* must be avoided, which there can be no difficulty in doing as it is above water: another rock, called *Noah's Ark*, is much closer in, but sufficiently distinguished by its bulk. Vessels anchor about five hundred yards from *Simon's Town*, which contains about thirty houses: it was garrisoned at the time we entered, by about five hundred of the 83d Infantry. Only a few vessels can obtain the necessary supplies at this place, provisions being brought from the interior at a very extravagant rate; a very small load requiring sixteen oxen to draw it through the sands. Forty dollars were asked for a horse-waggon to go to *Cape Town*, and ten for a saddle horse.—It ought not to be omitted to mention, that the black drivers are most expert coachmen: they drive eight in hand,

and turn a corner in the neatest style, at a full t..—*False Bay* is always resorted to during the N. W. monsoon, where vessels ride completely sheltered from its effects. We found in it, among others, an *American* loaded with seal skins for the Canton market: they were procured at an island in 46° south latitude, and in the longitude of the *Mauritius*. These skins differed from those caught in *North America*, in having a very rich fur instead of hair: the master expected a profit of forty thousand dollars on his cargo. Seals, but of a bad quality, are in great numbers in *False Bay*.

The high ridge which runs from the *Table Land* to the *Cape of Good Hope*, has the appearance from the top of being perfectly insulated from the rest of *Africa:* the only connection is, as already described, by a low sandy neck about nine or ten miles in breadth. The two bays laid down on the same map may be easily traced as likely to have once been but one channel running north and south: the formation of the isthmus is not difficult to be accounted for, when the action of the winds on this part of the coast is considered: they always blow here in two and directly opposite directions, nearly up and down the bays, and with a violence equal to raising a sufficient quantity of matter from the bottom to form a bank strong enough to oppose the wind themselves; the N. W. monsoon may be supposed to have closed the head of *Table Bay*, and the S. E. that of *False Bay*. This theory is strongly supported by the nature of the flat itself, and the soundings in the two bays, which are all strongly assimilated, being fine sand and shells: it may be necessary to observe, likewise, that the neck exists where the high lands bounding it approach nearest each other.

On our leaving the *Cape*, Major General Grey, brother to Lord Howick, was commander of the forces, and administered the civil government until the arrival of Lord Caledon, who was daily expected from *England* to assume it. Besides the troops already noticed, there was in the colony a corps of Hottentots about six hundred strong: they were dressed in a grey jacket and white trowsers, and armed with rifles, in the use of which they are considered very expert.

CHAPTER VIII.

Passage to and Arrival at St. Helena.—*Some Account of the Island.*

WE sailed out of harbour in great spirits, looking forward to commence operations in three or four months in the eastern seas, and which we expected to be attended with advantages of the most beneficial nature to all parties engaged in the expedition. From what we could learn at the *Cape*, it did not appear likely that we were destined against the *Mauritius*, which was represented to be in too powerful a state of defence for our small force. *Batavia* was mentioned as the probable point of attack; but most persons felt inclined to think *Manilla* the spot against which we were to direct our operations. Leaving the *Cape*, therefore, under this persuasion, our surprize may be easily conceived to have been great, when we beheld the Admiral, on the first evening, hoist the signal to steer N.W. We at first imagined this course to be a feint for the deception of any vessels that might meet the fleet in this neighbourhood: but when the signal was made the second day to stand N. N. W. we were undeceived, and saw that we were not destined to double the *Cape of Good Hope.* Our flattering visions now vanished; and putting together the accounts we had learnt at the *Cape,* respecting the events on the *River Plata,* the dispatches brought by the Fly brig for General Craufurd, and some circumstances in the convoy which we had been at some loss to account for, there appeared not a shadow of doubt, but that our original destination had been changed. This was certainly a subject of regret to all parties, as we were anxious to have a new field to ourselves; instead of which we were about to enter one, where neither military glory, or personal advantage, could be obtained, for we supposed that after the capture of *Monte Video,* Sir Samuel Auchmuty would strain every nerve to obtain possession of *Buenos Ayres,* and that we would only arrive in time to secure this possession. It must, however, be observed, that we had conjecture alone for going to *Spanish America;* for the same mysterious silence prevailed as at our leaving *England;* a silence highly creditable to those acquainted with the object of the armament, particularly as it is rather unusual in our service.

It was not wandering far into the field of speculation by those who imagined that events in
Europe might have rendered it necessary for us
to secure the *Brazils*, in which service we would
very likely be employed, as in the most fit preparation for it: this idea was supported by our
apparent direction for *St. Helena*, which is more
in the way to the *Brazils*, from the *Cape*, than
to the *Rio de la Plata*. We found ourselves
involved in a labyrinth out of which our approach
to the coast of *America* would alone furnish a
clue to guide us.

We continued our course to the northward and
westward, with favorable weather and wind,
excepting on the 10th, when we had the wind
a-head: at this time we were in latitude 30° S.
it again became favorable on the ensuing day, and
led us into the S. E. trade, which we entered in
26° of latitude. The Flying Fish schooner left us
on the 9th, to prepare for our reception at *St.
Helena*, which we expected to reach by the 19th,
but having met with light winds as we advanced
within the Tropic, we did not get sight of the
island until the morning of the 20th: when within
about nine leagues we hove to for the night,
sending in one of the gun brigs. At day-light the
next day we stood round the eastern point of the

island, and anchored at noon opposite *James Town*, situated on the N. W. side. As we approached the island, several rocks were mistaken by us for vessels: even seamen were deceived by the resemblance. The ships stood close to the land, which is very bold, and the perpendicular face of one rock, under which we sailed, presented a magnificent appearance.

The anchoring ground is in the open road, but it is very well sheltered from the S. E. winds by the high cliffs. No vessels can approach it without bringing to at a heavy battery under the N. E. point of the island, and sending a boat on shore: that no vessels may plead ignorance of this regulation, the word "*boat*" is written in large characters on a board, in English, French, and Dutch.

James Town is the only one in the island, and is situated in a very narrow valley, affording no more than sufficient room for one street to follow its windings: the landing is at some steps cut in the rock under the N. E. cliff. Though this is the most accessible part of the island, it is bad enough, as was experienced by several officers, whose boat was upset by the swell of the sea, which is always high near the shore: fortunately no lives were lost, owing to the immediate assistance received from other boats. The sharks are so bold at this spot as to have pursued swimmers to the very edge of the steps. Leaving the steps, and passing along the face of the rock, a draw-bridge admits you into the rear of a strong battery extending across the mouth of the valley, and presenting a heavy direct and flanking fire: here are situated the Company's stores. Continuing along the rear of this battery for near two hundred yards, you are received, through a second gate, into the principal street: on the left is the Governor's residence, called the Castle, but which has no defence; here the public offices are held, and the accommodations are said to be excellent: to the right of the gate is the church, a small plain building. The houses, as the street is ascended, are built in a neat manner after the English taste, but mostly thatched: this favorable appearance does not hold long, for the upper part of the town bears a most wretched aspect. The barracks are situated about half way up; the General Hospital still further: this is said not to be conducted in such a manner as to promise recovery to its patients. The town also contains a play-house, but the performers had lately left the island. On each side of the valley roads are cut out of the rock, and secured with parapets: that to the right leads to a strong battery on the cliff, and to a castle built on the top of a conical hill, called *Castle Hill*: it likewise branches off to the different country houses, to which the principal part of the inhabitants retire, when there are no ships in the roadsted: these country seats are situated on the little green spots which are to be met with in the inflections of the upper parts of the island, and which are alone fertile. Except a few shrubs about these grounds, not the least appearance of a tree meets the eye, and we found wood so scarce as to be obliged to break up old gun carriages for fuel.

Stock of every description is scarce, and of course high in price. It is said to have become more so, since the *Cape* has fallen into our hands.

The Company's ships are sometimes detained here for a length of time before they can proceed homeward, as it does not always happen that they find sufficient convoy at this station, to secure their passage through the *North Atlantic*. It happened in 1805, that the China and Bengal ships met here, and remained for seventeen weeks; and the numbers that accompanied Admiral Rainier home amounted to forty-five, the largest India fleet that ever arrived at once in *England*.

While delayed at *St. Helena*, the passengers are obliged to provide for themselves on shore, an opportunity the inhabitants do not let pass by, to put money into their pockets by excessive charges.

The population of the island is said to amount to about two thousand whites of English descent, and half this number of slaves. The same disease which had afflicted the *Cape* inhabitants, also found its way here: the measles were making most dreadful ravages, cutting off whole families at once. We were obliged to prevent the landing of any of our soldiers, except a small guard to enforce this regulation.

Every part of the island which can be considered in the least accessible, is strongly covered with battery over battery. Should it ever fall into the hands of an enemy, it will certainly be owing to want of vigilance on the part of those entrusted with its defence, as it is impossible for ships to approach without exposure to destruction. Signal stations are placed round the whole island. The troops consist of the St. Helena Corps, nine hundred strong, and of three hundred artillery, all in the Company's service: Sir Home Popham took with him, on his passage to *Buenos Ayres*, about two hundred of them.

Part of the fleet having taken in their water at a cistern near the landing place, and the remainder at a spot about one mile and a half below, with a supply of spirits for consumption at a *future* period, the signal was made on the 25th, for all persons to repair to their ships. We weighed the ensuing afternoon, when salutes were exchanged between the men of war and the island: the Admiral having collected the convoy together, signal was made to steer west. There remained at anchor seven sail of Chinamen (under convoy of the Hughes frigate), two Bengal ships, two South Sea whalers, a Dane, and an American. The English ships were to be allowed to proceed on their voyage four days after us: the neutrals not until ten. The Spencer and Theseus had put in here after twelve day's sailing from the *Cape:* they left it again in four days, without taking any merchantmen with them.

CHAPTER IX.

Departure from St. Helena.—*Passage across the* South Atlantic, *and Arrival at* Monte Video, *in the* Rio de la Plata.

WE left ten sick in the island, in hopes of saving them to the service, as their recovery from dysentery was not expected in case of their remaining any longer at sea: the convoy had lost nine on the passage from the *Cape* from the same disorder. Two officers who were dismissed by the general court martial held at the *Cape* were also left here to find their passage home. The fate of these two gentlemen, and of one in particular, excited the commisseration of every person in the fleet: and it was lamented that clemency and military example could not have been blended in his case. The sentences of some other officers tried by the same court were not made known.

The General, in orders, particularly called upon the officers under his command to continue their exertions for securing the health of the troops

M

in the prosecution of the voyage ; and he observed that their attention to this subject was now of greater necessity than hitherto, as we had already been a long period at sea, and were about entering a climate (before disembarkation) in which we would most probably encounter very bad weather, and heavy rains. The lime juice which had been stopped on leaving *St. Jago* was again ordered to be issued in quantities at the discretion of the officer commanding each ship, and additional supplies were served out from the store ships.

We were somewhat surprised on the 28th, at having the wind from the west for some time, and likewise from the south, as we looked for very little variation from the S. E. trade. We never found the N. E. trade on the other side of the equator vary but between that point and the east; whereas, until we had got as far south and west as in latitude 18° and longitude 13°, after leaving *St. Helena*, the winds frequently deviated eight points and was light, seldom carrying us above four and half knots : after this the trade became more settled, and we went six, seven, and eight and a half knots. We had got on the 1st of *May* into 15° west, when the Saracen gun brig left us under a press of sail, and on the 6th. we crossed our old track on the passage to the *Cape*, and about that spot where we had been on the 13th of *February*. We little expected at that time to have re-visited this climate so soon again : and we should have then considered an assertion to this effect as a desperate one indeed. Though we sailed over this track before in doubt, yet our hopes were high, whereas our feelings were now of a different nature : those prospects of active service which kept us in such good spirits formerly, no longer affected us, and the humble prospect of garrison duty alone struck our imaginations. The only relief we felt from such reflections was in the chance of being employed at the *Brazils;* for, our continuing so much to the westward, justified in some measure an opinion to this effect. If this should be the case, in what character were we to appear? in an hostile or friendly one? We recollected Earl St. Vincent's and General Simcoe's joint mission to *Lisbon;* but with the nature of it, the public had never been made acquainted. *Rio Janeiro* and *St. Salvador*, the two chief places in the *Brazils,* were well fortified; and it was doubted whether our force was adequate to taking and keeping possession of either, in opposition to the Portuguese government; and their jealousy of the

---

presence of strangers in their American colonies was well known to us.—Again, if we were bound to *Buenos Ayres*, why take so circuitous a route? Surely, if the distress of our army serving there, was so great as represented, it was cruel to lose one moment in affording it relief; and it appeared that delay certainly arose from taking *St. Helena* in our route: for, by the accounts of several who had made the passage from the *Cape of Good Hope* to that of *St. Mary*, it did not appear necessary to stand so far to the northward.

These were the questions daily agitated; and the more we entered into the discussion, the more we found ourselves bewildered.

At day light on the 8th, we got sight of the small island of *Trinidad*, situated about six hundred miles east of *Cape Frio*. We passed near five leagues to the southward of it. It is high in the middle, sinking gradually in a broken line to the sea: its east end presents a rock rising perpendicularly like a tower to the height of near one hundred and fifty feet; the base appearing equal to one third of its height, and no artificial work could shew a more regular form at the distance from which we viewed it. This island belongs to the Portuguese; and we were informed by some sailors of that nation, that there were some inhabitants on it, and that it was well stocked with cattle: it is very bold, and has a good anchorage at a small port, called *Port Navigation*, on the east side of the island. We encountered rainy squalls in this neighbourhood, both in *February* and *May*, and it may therefore be supposed such weather is frequent here.— The *Saracen* rejoined us as we passed, having come forward with the view of ascertaining the true position of *Trinidada*, which was found to be in lat. 20° 33′ S. and 29° 17′ W. longitude; this latter was the mean of several chronometers: Heather, in his chart, lays it down eighteen miles farther north, and twenty-three west.

The winds now began to vary, blowing from the south, S.S.E. and N.E. in which latter it remained from the 12th to the 16th, carrying us at seven, eight, and nine knots, with clear weather. The Saracen again left us on the 14th, when we received orders to be prepared for defence against privateers, in case of separation before reaching *Rio de la Plata*, a destination no longer considered necessary to be kept secret: we had altered our course to the southward some days back.— A hazy atmosphere, and strong flashes of lightning in the S. W. were the forerunners of a change of wind, which headed us on the 16th. when in 29° of lat. and in long. 49°, and which likewise brought us wet weather. From this day we experienced very little variation in wind and weather: the former appeared well settled in the south and west, points from whence it almost constantly blows in the three winter months, whereas in summer it prevails in the N. E. and N.W. By the 22d we had lost fifteen miles, and had during this time approached within seventy miles of the land, without seeing it. Two strange sail appeared on the 16th, of which only one was spoken, and proved a brig that had been driven out of *Porto Pedro*.

We continued beating to the southward until the evening of the 23d, when we stood our course with the wind at S. E. A sudden squall about two in the morning rendered our main-top mast useless; but in about thirty-six hours a new one was got up, and sail set on it: we were in the mean time towed by the Africa. We continued with fine weather, and a fair wind, until the 27th, when we made *Cape St. Maria*, in the N.W. As we stood for the river, the wind suddenly blew from the S.W. which obliged us to bring up to the westward of the cape, the island of *Lobos* bearing S.W. by W. six leagues. We had sixteen and a half fathoms soft muddy bottom, which proved very bad holding ground; for the wind blowing strong during the night, most of the ships drove, and some parted from their anchors: as the wind blew along the coast, no danger attended this weather.

On making the land we were joined by two frigates and a sloop of war, that had been cruizing for some time at the mouth of the river. We learnt from them that Lieutenant-General Whitelocke had arrived from *England* to take the command of the troops; and that every thing was in preparation at *Monte Video* to proceed, on our arrival, against *Buenos Ayres*, which was still in the hands of the Spaniards.

On the evening of the 1st of June it again blew violently from the S.W. our ship was so strained as to upset all the pawls of the windlass. Whenever this wind blew strong, it brought showers with it.

The Admiral determined upon weighing on the 4th of June, which the fleet did in the morning, with the wind at W. by N. and smooth water. We stood close hauled on the starboard tack until two, when we put about for the land. The wind had gradually come round to the south, blowing fresher, and bringing with it a thick fog, which rendered the land invisible to us until about dusk, when we could just descry it, and then put about; at this time the whole fleet, excepting a frigate, was to windward, and barely discernible. The sky bore a most unfavorable aspect, and threatened a storm, in which we were not deceived; for about midnight the wind had encreased to one of the most dreadful gales that had yet been experienced since leaving *England*. It was not possible for us to carry more sail than what was necessary to keep the ship to, with the helm lashed down. The sea ran terribly high, and poured into the crevices of our ports and scuttles so as to keep the pumps at work during the whole gale. We anxiously looked for a return of day, in hopes that we should be relieved from a very unpleasant situation, the horrors of which were not a little encreased by knowing that our vessel was old and crazy, and her pumps in such a state as to require clearing of sand and dirt every hour: she had besides shifted her ballast to leeward. At day light the gale blew with encreased fury, there were only three transports in company, and the troops were starving with wet and cold: at noon the appearance of the sky improved to windward. and the night was less violent than the former. We had been driving to the N. E. and supposed ourselves about twenty-five leagues east of *Lobos.* The wind was still fresh, on the 6th, from the S. S. W. but as the sea had moderated we wore ship, and an observation gave us 34° 34′ latitude. We hoped that the moon, which was renewed this evening, would produce a change in the weather; and were not disappointed, for on the 7th the sea was smooth, and the wind from the S. E. which in the evening blew from the N. E. We were now about one hundred and twenty miles from *Cape St. Mary;* the weather was warm, and a fine clear atmosphere. The ship only sailed at two knots during the night, but in the morning we were carried at eight and nine knots under reefed top-sails. We were however baulked in our expectations of making *Maldonado* before night, as the wind failed us; we could only get sight of the cone at sun-set from our main-rigging: the coast had been in view since morning.

We were about dark thrown into no small alarm by a sail bearing down upon us from the land, and which appeared when within a mile not to belong to the convoy, an opinion one of the officers had all along maintained against that of his brother officers. As she excited suspicion by

N

her manner, it was thought adviseable to be prepared against a surprize: our guns were loaded, matches lighted, and a proportion of the men placed on the deck with arms. We hove to, and waited her approach, which was made in a manner to increase our suspicions. When within fifty yards we hailed each other: the stranger answered that he was from *Monte Video*, with dispatches for our Admiral: several other questions were put to him, which were by no means answered in a satisfactory manner, and after crossing our bows and stern he laid close along our weather quarter, which we expected to be followed up by a broadside, and were ready to answer him in a warm style. Some further conversation having ensued, a voice on board the strange sail was recognized to be that of one of our officers serving at *Monte Video*. He immediately came on board, and informed us he had been some time in search of the Admiral, and had only yet met with another transport besides us: he gave us nothing new respecting the operations on shore, and left us again in the evening.

We stood the whole night S. W. by S. and put about the next morning, when we got sight of land at ten; but it was impossible to ascertain our position, the atmosphere was so dense about the horizon. We got about noon within two miles of the shore, and directly opposite some habitations of an inferior description: there were inhabitants about them, and very extensive herds of cattle feeding as far as our glasses could assist the view. On putting about, the wind favored us so as to allow us to weather the island of *Lobos* about eight in the evening, but, falling in with a current as we opened the river, we did not make such progress up as expected. At day-light we stood in for *Maldonado*, the harbour of which we approached very close before putting about: a counter-current favoring us in shore, we did not make stretches above five or six miles from it. One or two vessels that had entered the river with ourselves always brought up at night; but as we had an excellent chart of the soundings and shoals we kept under weigh until making *Monte Video*, on the 12th of June, where we anchored about three miles and a half from the mouth of the harbour. One vessel only came in at the same time, and it was the 14th before the remainder of the convoy arrived. They had, during the gale of the 5th, kept to windward, and on the change

N 2

of the 8th, found themselves far to the southward of *Cape St. Mary :* they were obliged to beat in, until being a little favored by the winds, they entered by the passage south of the *English Bank.*

END OF PART I.

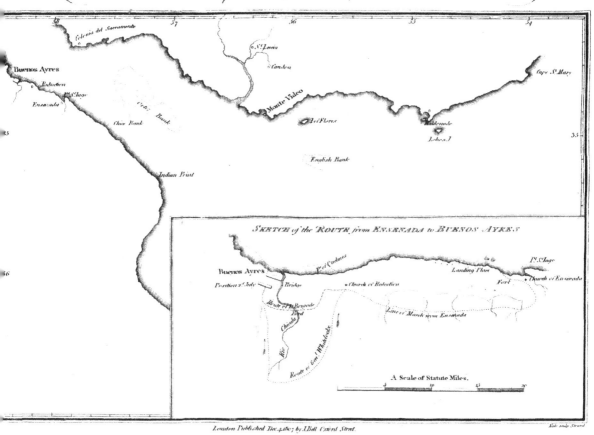

Sketch of
(RIO de la PLATA *from Cape St. Mary to* BUENOS AYRES.)

Buenos Ayres

Colonia del Sacramento

St. Lucia

Canelou

Monte Video

Isl. Flores

Cape St. Mary

Maldonado

Lobos I.

Reduction

Pta. S. Iago

Ensenada

Ortiz Bank

Chico Bank

English Bank

Indian Point

SKETCH of the ROUTE from ENSENADA to BUENOS AYRES.

Buenos Ayres

Pta. of Cudmes

Landing Place

Pta. S. Iago

Position 2d. July

Bridge

Church of Reduction

Fort

Church of Ensenada

Route of Br. under Brig. Chiesa

Line of March from Ensenada

Riac

Route of Gen. Whitelock

A Scale of Statute Miles.

London Published Dec. 4. 1807 by J. Bell Oxford Street.

PART II.

—

CHAPTER I.

Brief Account of the Transactions against General Beresford, after the Capture of Buenos Ayres in 1806.—Arrival of Reinforcements from the Cape and from England. —Advance of these against Monte Video.

Before proceeding to treat of the movements of Sir Samuel Auchmuty's little army and General Craufurd's, now united under the command of Lieutenant-General Whitelocke, it may not be amiss to take a short retrospect of the transactions on the *River Plata* before this period.

It is well known how Brigadier-General Beresford and Commodore Sir Home Popham had, with the very small force of seventeen hundred men, taken possession of *Buenos Ayres* on the

25th of June, 1806. Aware of the precarious situation in which he found himself in the midst of a numerous population, and in an open place, or at best in a fortress not tenable, General Beresford immediately forwarded to the *Cape of Good Hope* an application for reinforcements, until a sufficient army to retain possession could be sent from *England*. The line of conduct he adopted towards the inhabitants was of a conciliatory nature, though, at the same time, he established a strong police for the preservation of good order, and to watch any movements of a suspicious nature. The surprize by which the American Spaniards had been struck at the first view of English troops, where they had never been seen before, soon wore away; and they were not long in discovering the great advantages they would have in a well conducted insurrection against the invaders. The Vice-roy had fled; but there remained men of sufficient consequence to excite a party against the English, and the support they could obtain from *Monte Video*, in men and arms, was far from being of a trifling nature. Accordingly, a man of the name of Pueridon, having got together about fifteen hundred men, advanced with nine field pieces against *Buenos Ayres :* General Beresford, with five hundred men, met him about twelve miles from the town, dispersed the insurgents, and brought back in triumph the whole of their artillery.

A much more formidable attack was, however, preparing at *Colonia del Sacramento*, about thirty miles on the opposite bank of the *Rio de la Plata*. At this place had been assembled a large force, and a supply of arms and ammunition: a great number of small vessels had been collected to carry this armament across the river; and a favorable opportunity was alone wanting for this purpose. The command had been entrusted to a French gentleman of the name of Linier, but who had been bred in the Spanish marine, and resided for many years past in *South America*. General Beresford had apprized Sir Home Popham of the preparations made to attack him, and this officer, in consequence, sailed up from his cruizing ground at the mouth of the river, and arrived opposite to *Buenos Ayres* on the 1st of August. One of the north-easterly gales prevented his being able to land before the next day; and reimbarking on the 5th. During this time several of his armed launches sunk at their moorings. The Spaniards took advantage of this gale to effect their passage across the river; and knowing the effects of it in swelling its waters, they passed over the bank called *Palmas*, about nine miles above *Buenos Ayres*. Violent rains had set in with the gales, the roads were much damaged, and this circumstance, added to the danger of quitting the town in its present ferment, General Beresford found himself reduced to the necessity of concentrating his defence to the castle and adjacent square.

Linier was reinforced at his landing by parties from all quarters: he moved on towards *Buenos Ayres*, occupied the *Miserere*, or slaughtering-place, and on the 10th of August took possession of *El Retiro*. He, notwithstanding his great superiority in numbers, advanced cautiously into the town: and when Sir Home Popham landed on the 11th, he found General Beresford defending with obstinacy the approaches to the *Great Square;* but the enemy, assisted by the inhabitants within, gradually gained ground in the streets, and lodged themselves in the commanding houses. It was now deemed adviseable to attempt a retreat across the small river *Chiculo,* and gain *Ensenada,* whence a reimbarkation might be effected. The wounded, and some treasure, were first conveyed over; but before any further progress could be made with the few boats in our possession, the Spaniards, who had become masters of all the avenues, opposed it, and Sir Home himself with difficulty escaped to his own vessel. The attack upon the *Square* was again renewed in the morning; our troops were forced into the Castle, and this being under the command of the neighbouring houses, now possessed by the enemy, General Beresford was obliged to surrender. There were two hundred and fifty of his little army killed and wounded; the remainder were made prisoners of war, consisting of a few dragoons and artillery, the 71st Regiment of Infantry, and about one hundred and fifty of the *St. Helena* Corps; the whole amounted to about fourteen hundred. The few who had escaped across the *Chieulo*, and were seamen, carried the news of the disastrous event to *Ensenada*, whence they had the good fortune to provide for their escape, after spiking the guns, and rendering them otherwise useless.

Sir Home Popham now proceeded with the little squadron under his command to the mouth of the *Rio*, to wait for the expected reinforcements from the *Cape*. The first of them appeared on the 5th of October, and seven days after, the whole detachment arrived under the command of Lieutenant-Colonel Backhouse of the 47th Infantry. It consisted of two squadrons of the 20th

O

Light Dragoons, one company of Artillery, the 38th and 47th Regiments of Infantry, and a company of the 54th Infantry that had been recovered from the French on board the Volontaire frigate. This armament sailed up to *Monte Video*, in the expectation of being able, by a co-operative attack of the land and sea forces, to get possession; but it was found impossible to bring the men of war sufficiently near to cover the landing of the troops, or to make any impression on the town. It was now deemed adviseable to secure some post on the river, where the detachment could maintain itself until the arrival of additional reinforcements from *England*, which it was naturally expected would be delayed as little as possible. The town of *Maldonado*, situated at the mouth of the river, was well calculated for this purpose; it could supply the necessary refreshments for the troops, and its harbour would prove an excellent rendezvous for the cruizers. The squadron came to anchor off this place on the 29th, and the troops were landed in the afternoon: the distance from the beach to the town is about one mile, and a body of Spaniards were drawn up in front of it, with some light artillery, which they directed at our troops advancing towards them: they were, however, soon daunted by the resolute and firm approach of the English, and retired into the town, which very soon after surrendered by capitulation. In the mean time, Sir Home Popham had summoned the small island of *Goritti*, which is within the harbour, and defends it by very heavy batteries. Those guarding these works, finding resistance would be vain, yielded and became prisoners of war. Here the detachment remained until the arrival of Sir Samuel Auchmuty.

This gallant officer had sailed from *Falmouth* on the 11th of October, under convoy of the Ardent, 64, with four squadrons of the 17th Light Dragoons, some artillery, the 40th and 87th Regiments of Infantry, and three companies of the Rifle Corps. He arrived at *Rio Janeiro*, in the *Brazils*, on the 14th of December, and having refreshed his troops for a week, during which time the convoy was likewise watered, he continued his voyage, and reached the *River Plate* on the 5th of January. No time was lost in reimbarking the troops at *Maldonado*; and the works in the neighbourhood having been dismantled, the army sailed on the 10th against *Monte Video*. Rear-Admiral Stirling, who had superseded Sir Home Popham on this station, commanded the naval force employed on the occasion. On the morning of the 16th a landing was effected at some rocks about eight miles below the town. No opposition was made to this movement, except by a cannonade at a very long range, from a strong body of the enemy, who viewed it at a distance, and did not think it prudent to present any other obstacle. Three days after this, Sir Samuel advanced towards the place, and, on the march, was attacked by about four thousand mounted Spaniards with artillery; but they were soon forced to retire, and with very little loss on our part. In the evening a commanding position was assumed just without the range of the guns of *Monte Video*.

On the morning of the 20th, a sortie was made from the garrison with a view of dislodging the English from their position. The Spaniards marched out in two columns to the number of about six thousand, advanced against our force with intrepidity, and fought with some determination. The right column first gave way, but that on the left continued the attack with great obstinacy, and were opposed with like gallantry by the piquet composed of detachments from the different regiments, and commanded by Major Campbell, of the 40th, until they were charged in front and flank by the light battalion, when they were broken, and fled into the town, leaving on the spot about three hundred dead, and as many prisoners : their wounded managed to regain the place. In this column, which had fought with some spirit, were their marine troops, and a great number of Frenchmen.—The gallant little English army obtained this victory at the price of only twenty-five killed, and about one hundred wounded. Every corps behaved bravely, but the rifle corps particularly distinguished themselves. This was the first opportunity they had met with, since their formation, of proving their utility; and the manner in which they conducted themselves excited as much admiration on the part of their companions in arms, as it did dread among their enemies : this character they maintained afterwards on all occasions. At the time this action was fought, the Vice-roy was approaching with a lage force, and only removed about ten miles. Hearing of the defeat of the garrison, he faced about and retired, leaving it to its own defence. Sir Samuel now commenced establishing batteries against the citadel and town, a brief description of which will be necessary to illustrate the operations of the siege.

CHAPTER II. *(Vide Plate.)*

Description of the Town of Monte Video.— *Assault.—Transactions from this Period until the Arrival of General Crawfurd's Army.*

THE town of *Monte Video*, situated on the north side of the *Rio de la Plata*, is about eighty miles above *Cape St. Mary*, and takes its name from a conical hill on the opposite side of the harbour, which is to the westward and northward. It is built on a rocky ridge running into the bason in form of a peninsula, fortified all round, but only on the land side in any degree after the modern system of defence. On this side it appears to have had originally but a stone wall, about four feet thick and fifteen high, to which have been added, in the centre of the line, a square fort, called the citadel, and along it some strong redoubts in the form of demi-bastions, mounted with heavy ordnance, and in an excellent state of defence. The curtains co necting these are in their original state, no addition appearing to have

MONTE VIDEO.

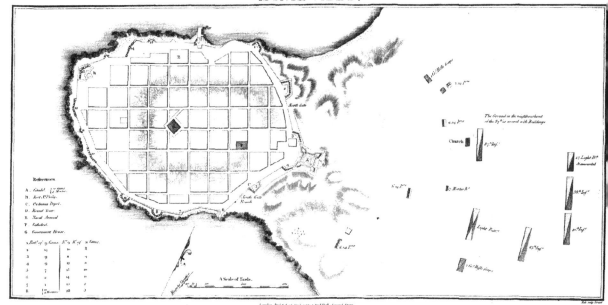

A Scale of Yards.

London Published Dec.r 4.1807 by Bell Bell Jones & Sons.

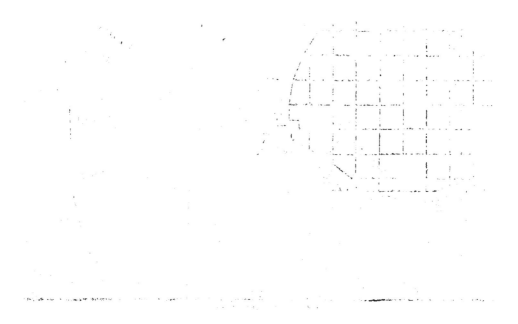

been made. The citadel is a regular work with bastions, a ditch, and a small revelin covering the face towards the country, the whole rivetted with brick: its glacis is in a very broken state, and the only entrance is within the town, over a draw-bridge.—There are two entrances into the town from the country, one on each side of the citadel: the north gate is in the curtain next removed from it: the south gate is in that face nearest the river, from which it is distant about one hundred yards: it leads through a single wall; but is strongly covered by the guns of the demi-bastion, which is made the great depot for naval ordnance, and two guns of large calibre on a round tower near the water. From this tower, the defences follow the shape of the tongue on which *Monte Video* is built; these consist of very heavy sea batteries connected by a covered way. A small enclosed fort, named after St. Philip, covers the most important of these batteries, which are also difficult of approach, from the rocky nature of the shore. The only landing place is within the harbour at a stone pier. The cathedral is a large brick building, with two lofty square towers and a cupola, and is placed in the western face of an open square, near the citadel: there is a second church belonging to the Dominicians. the only order of monks in this town. The streets are laid out at right angles, in lots of about one hundred feet in each face, and occupied with brick houses, having flat roofs, and parapets of four feet in height surrounding them : the windows are grated with iron, a precaution necessary in a climate, where too much air cannot be admitted, and where also a great number of the inhabitants subsist by depredations on their neighbours.— The ground on the outside of the town is much broken by the gullies formed when the excessive rains set in at particular seasons : this space was occupied by several small houses, which were demolished at the approach of our troops : one of a larger description only was left, about six hundred yards from the place, and which served as good cover for part of our troops employed at the batteries.

Several twenty-four pounders having been disembarked from the men of war, a battery of six guns, and a second of four guns, and one mortar, were established against the citadel : another of equal force was raised against the south gate, and on the prolongation of the lower flank of the demi-bastion protecting it ; it battered in breach about ten yards below the gate, and at the distance of about six hundred yards. Two guns were also established against the gun-boats which the enemy might bring close to the beach in the harbour, to annoy the right of our position. They began to play on the 21st of January; a great number of shot were directed at the outer face of the S.E. bastion, the merlons of which were nearly destroyed, but without any appearance of effecting a practicable breach at this place. The lower battery proved more effectual against its object, besides laying open the angle of the demi-bastion opposed to it, which exposed its guns to our enfilading fire, but from which they do not appear to have suffered. The wall near the gate soon exhibited symptoms of demolition, and on the 2d of February it was declared practicable: It would have been a desirable object to have silenced the six guns flanking it; but a great quantity of ammunition having been expended against the citadel, which it had never been intended to assault, a scarcity now existed, nor could the men of war encrease the supply. Sir Samuel therefore determined on losing no time to get possession by force, and he issued the necessary orders for every preparation to be made to storm the place the next morning, in case a summons which he sent to the Governor in the evening should not be attended with the desired effect. Receiving no answer to

P

his message, the troops proceeded to the assault about three o'clock on the morning of the 3d of February. The principal attack was against the breach at the south gate, while another column was directed against the works on the north side of the citadel, where it was to scale the walls, and proceeding to the left along the rear of the lines, was to form a junction with those who should force the breach and incline to the right.

The left column had to proceed over very broken ground, and it advanced in dead silence towards the breach. The forlorn hope had nearly arrived under the redoubt, when a discharge was made from its artillery, by which only one man was struck: it now pushed forward to the breach, followed by a second party of thirty, twenty-five of whom were levelled to the ground at the second discharge. The light battalion now pressing forward, reached the breach, which only afforded the ascent of three men abreast: here every exertion was required to force a passage, which was at last effected, but with a dreadful loss, above four hundred in killed and wounded being left on this spot, against which was concentrated the whole fire of the enemy from the depot, and from the two guns on the round tower. Once within the breach, the Spaniards fled before our troops, who, turning to the right, put to the bayonet every man found in the rear of the works: they attained the bastion under the citadel, where the Governor had stationed himself, and who refused to survive the disgrace of losing the town, though repeated offers were made to spare him : he received a musket ball in the breast, and a stroke of a bayonet in his only arm. The carnage here was dreadful, every Spaniard being bayoneted on the spot. Major Campbell of the 40th, with the grenadiers of the 38th and 87th, after entering the breach, filed to the left, and carried, at the point of the bayonet, the different batteries that lie between it and *Fort St. Philip.*

During this time the right column, consisting of one company of the Rifle Corps and the 87th Infantry, advanced to the walls near the north gate. Part of the Rifle Corps scaled, and the gates being forced open from within, the remainder entered and turned to the left towards the citadel, which still pretended to hold out, though the town was now completely in possession of our troops. Some riflemen reached the cathedral, and ascended its towers, whence they had an entire command of the works of the citadel, from which they soon dislodged the enemy. About half past eight it surrendered at discretion, and Sir Samuel Auchmuty found himself master of the object, which his own gallantry and that of his army gave them every title to have possession of.

On this occasion, every thing was done on the part of our troops by the bayonet: with this weapon they killed above seven hundred and fifty of the enemy: about two thousand were taken prisoners, and the remainder of the garrison effected their escape by means of their communications with *Rat Island*, which it would have been no difficult task for our navy to have cut off. Among the prisoners was the Governor, a Frenchman: he survived but a few hours, and was universally lamented by both parties: it had been the wish of our officers to save the life of this brave man, who, from the circumstance of having lost a hand in some former engagement, was better known by the appellation of *Maincourt*, than by his real name *Mordelle*.

The joy of effecting this conquest was not a little damped by the reflection that it had been purchased with the blood of a great number of gallant men, and particularly of officers. This slaughter had been entirely occasioned by the fire of the guns in the depot, which commanded the breach within eighty yards, and disgorged from large calibres grape and landgridge in perfect

109

showers : whole sections were brought to the ground at a volley. Had one half the quantity of shot, which had been uselessly expended against the citadel, been employed in silencing these guns, the place would have been obtained at one third the loss. The skill employed in this siege does not appear to have equalled the intrepidity exhibited on the occasion.

Three days after the fall of *Monte Video*, the Nereide frigate arrived with the 9th Light Dragoons, which had parted from General Craufurd's army at *St. Jago.*

On the first appearance of the English reinforcements, General Linier, who had assumed the command of the Spanish forces, removed the prisoners who had been taken with General Beresford, about three hundred miles into the interior of the country, and the men were separated from the officers. General Beresford remonstrated; but these remonstrances proved fruitless; for though General Linier felt inclined to an exchange of prisoners, yet this was very strongly opposed by the civil authorities. The Spanish forces were recruited, and even received parties of men from the opposite side of the continent, chiefly consisting of volunteers, natives of *Old Spain*, and who proved their best soldiers. There, were, besides, a number of Frenchmen in the province, the most respectable of whom were employed as officers, and others in disciplining the inhabitants whom he had prevailed on, by various measures, to take up arms in their defence: it is perhaps not necessary to add, that religion proved the most powerful engine he could employ on this occasion.

After gaining possession of *Monte Video*, Sir Samuel Auchmuty detached parties into the country, to watch any attempts on the part of the enemy, and to protect the inhabitants who could be encouraged to bring supplies to the markets. *Canalon*, about twenty miles above the garrison, was occupied by a detachment of two hundred men; and another was posted at *St. Lucie*, about twenty miles further. The Light Battalion, with the three companies of the Rifle Corps, were sent in vessels to possess themselves of *Colonia del Sacramento*, only thirty miles on the opposite side to *Buenos Ayres*, and which they effected on the 5th of March, without opposition. The enemy at different times attempted to disturb these posts; but with very little success: their attempts seemed to be particularly directed against *Colonia*. On one occasion, the 20th of March, they approached, and drove in the outposts about midnight. The alarm was given, and the piquet moved out to keep them in check, until the garrison could stand to their arms. A few shot having been directed at the enemy from some works that had been raised by our troops, they retired, and were preserved from a pursuit by the darkness of the night.

Emboldened by their security in their approaches to *Colonia*, a more serious attack was designed against it by two thousand of their choicest troops, who were crossed over from *Buenos Ayres*, under the command of one of their most able officers. On the 6th of June this corps encamped at *St. Pedro*, about fourteen miles above *Colonia*, where Lieutenant-Colonel Pack, of the 71st Infantry, now commanded. This officer had been made prisoner with General Beresford, and had also the good fortune to escape with his gallant chief. Having been apprized of the approach of the Spaniards, he determined upon not waiting for them, but leaving *Colonia* with his little army early on the morning of the 7th, he arrived at day-light within view of the enemy, drawn up on the opposite side of a small river. Our troops instantly forded it, where they could only form in sections, and advanced briskly to the charge. The Spanish cavalry soon turned about; but their infantry appeared determined to meet the English bayonet, a view of which, however, at the distance of eighty yards, appalled them, and, after giving their fire, they fled in all directions, throwing away their arms and accoutrements, that they might not be encumbered in their flight from our brave fellows, who endeavoured to overtake them; but as they were much fatigued by the preceding march, only one hundred prisoners were made, among whom was the second in command of the Spanish corps. One standard, and the whole of their artillery, consisting of six field pieces, fell into the hands of the victors. We had only two men killed on this occasion, but several were afterwards wounded by the accidental explosion of one of the tumbrils, after it had fallen into our hands. Colonel Pack returned in the evening to *Colonia*, after performing an exploit, which carries with it its own eulogium.

On the 10th of May the Thisbe frigate arrived at *Monte Video*. She brought out Lieutenant-General Whitelocke as Commander in Chief of the British Forces in *South America;* and Major General Gower came with him as second in command. They had sailed from *England* on the 9th of March, with several transports, having on board the 89th Regiment of Infantry, a detachment of flying artillery, and a number of recruits for the regiments on this station: a small proportion of the flying artillery were in the Thisbe. The arrival of these troops, as well as of those under General Craufurd, was now anxiously looked for. Some unaccountable contradiction appears to have existed respecting this officer's armament: it had been expected by Sir Samuel Auchmuty, and on *official authority*, at the time he only received the 9th Light Dragoons. Yet, it can scarcely be credited that General Craufurd should have directed his course to the eastward after leaving *St. Jago*, had he been instructed to touch, in his way to his ultimate destination, at *Monte Video*, in order to assist Sir Samuel, in case he should stand in need of it.

Colonel Mahon, of the 9th Light Dragoons, was detached, on the morning of the 12th of June, with five hundred men, to support Lieutenant-Colonel Backhouse, who was stationed at *Canalon* with two hundred. This officer had been summoned to surrender on the former day by a particular hour, or that he should be attacked by fourteen hundred men, who were ready to follow up the summons: he thought it prudent to retire, and was met near *Monte Video* by Colonel Mahon, who took back with him the two field pieces belonging to the retreating party. The Spaniards, apprized of the approach of Colonel Mahon, retired, and this officer not being able to come up with them, returned on the 14th.

CHAPTER III.

Preparations to sail against Buenos Ayres.—
Departure from Monte Video.—*Arrival at*
Colonia del Sacramento.—*Landing at* Ense-
nada.—*March from thence to* Reduction.

THE newly arrived troops were supplied with
every refreshment the place could afford : these
consisted of fresh meat and vegetables, which were
obtained at a most reasonable rate : bread was
not so plentiful, but excellent.

Every preparation was now making to proceed
with all expedition against *Buenos Ayres.* The
troops who were to join us at *Monte Video* were
embarking, and those already embarked were
shifted on board vessels not drawing above thirteen
feet water. This measure of course crowded
the ships to double the number of men, according
to their tonnage; but as the voyage was to be a
short one, it was very cheerfully submitted to.
On the 16th, a Spanish field officer arrived with a
flag of truce from *Buenos Ayres,* the first received
by us since in possession of *Monte Video.* His
avowed mission was, to effect an exchange of three

of our officers, in their possession, for three Spaniards of equal rank; but there existed little doubt,
that his chief object was to obtain some knowledge
of our force and preparations, particularly as he
named three Spanish gentlemen, in exchange, who
had been ordered to *England :* he returned the
next morning. The three English officers had
fallen into the hands of the Spaniards by a
stratagem which deserves to be recorded. They
had been in the habit of visiting some ladies at
St. Lucie, where they were stationed, and a
meeting was appointed with them on a particular
evening, about three miles from their quarters.
While engaged with the fair ones, the house was
surrounded by a number of armed men, and the
English gentlemen carried off, thus falling into
iron fetters instead of the silken bands of love.
Some naval officers had also been seized on,
while in chace of other game.

The harbour of *Monte Video* was literally
crowded with shipping : it bore the appearance
of a winter forest. Above thirty of the vessels
were merchantmen, laid up here until our gaining
possession of *Buenos Ayres* should enable them
to proceed for that market, as it was impossible
to dispose of their cargoes at this place. The
merchants, and other British subjects, were formed
into a corps, about four hundred strong, and

undergoing a course of drilling, so as to be qualified to assist at the defence of the works, in case of an attack after the army should have proceeded for the capital. These had been put into a temporary state of repair : the south gate was closed up, and strengthened in the rear ; and behind the wall, where the breach had been effected, a strong rampart was commenced, and rivetted within with brick. The command of the garrison was entrusted to Colonel Brown, of the 40th, an active and vigilant officer ; one company of artillery, two squadrons of dragoons, the 47th Infantry, and a party of marines, were deemed sufficient to defend *Monte Video* against any attempt, while the army acted against *Buenos Ayres.*

Owing to the winds and other causes, it was so late as the 17th of June, before the first division of the troops embarked could get under weigh, and the progress made before night was not much : at dusk the vessels came to an anchor about seven miles from the mouth of the harbour. This division was commanded by Sir Samuel Auchmuty, who was on board the Saracen sloop of war brig, which, with another armed brig and schooner, made our convoy. We were to rendezvous at *Colonia,* from whence we were to cross over the *Rio de la Plata,* after re-embarking the light battalion and other troops serving there. Orders had been issued to take the passage south of the *Ortiz Bank*, which had been marked out with beacons at the principal points; and instructions for this navigation had been previously issued to the masters of transports. On the 21st we had made but little way, owing to our having encountered light and baffling winds: this day we got sight of the rear division of transports with the remainder of the army on board, at about seven or eight miles to the N. E. Assisted by the tides, we got up sufficiently far on the 22d, to get a view of the beacon on the *Ortiz Bank :* but we could proceed no farther until the 24th, when a strong breeze having set in early from the N. E. we passed the channel between the above mentioned and the *Chica Banks,* and anchored off *Colonia* about three in the afternoon: we had lost sight of the rear division. The Haughty gun brig arrived at the same time, with six gun-boats in tow, formerly captured from the Spaniards, and now destined to co-operate in the attack on their capital. General Gower came in, in the evening, and hurried the embarkation of the troops, which was effected the next day. *Colonia* was left without a British soldier, and the few guns in the place were ordered to be rendered unserviceable.

An order was sent for us to join the main body

of the army at anchor about twelve miles to the
S. E. where it had arrived on the 24th, but it was
impossible for us to proceed on the 25th, owing
to the thickness of the fog, which was such as to
prevent our seeing any object at a ship's length.
Before leaving this place a new arrangement of
the brigades became necessary, as in the former
distribution made at *Monte Video*, the arrival of
Brigadier General Auckland and Colonel Lord
Blaney had been calculated upon, and the wind
for some time had given us reason to expect them
hourly with the reinforcement under their command.   By this last arrangement the troops were
brigaded in the following order :

Lieutenant-General Whitelocke,
Commander in Chief.

Major-General Gower,
Second in Command.

Light Brigade,   Brig.-Gen. Craufurd.

Light Batt. 9 Comp. 8 Comp. Rifle Corps

The Hon. Col. Mahon.   Brig. Gen. Lumley.   Sir Sam. Auchmuty.

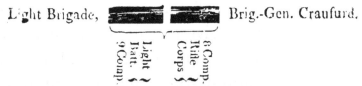

Dismounted 9th Light Dragoons 4 Squadrons — 45th Infantry. — 40th Infantry. — 9 Squ. dismount. Carabineers. — 88th Infantry. — 36th Infantry. — 4 Squ. 17 Drag. dismounted — 87th Infantry. — 38th Infantry. — 5th Infantry.

Two companies ■ Royal Artillery.

There were a few mounted dragoons as orderlies, and to the light brigade were attached two light three pounders. It is however necessary to observe, that this order of battle was not much attended to, either on the march, or in presence of the place of attack : the troops moved as most suited the conveniency of the moment, and indeed it became at times completely inverted.

We sailed from *Colonia* on the morning of the 26th, and about noon joined the remainder of the fleet standing up the river, close hauled on the starboard tack, under convoy of the Nereide frigate, on board of which Admiral Murray's flag was flying. There were three other frigates in company, besides four gun-brigs, three armed schooners, and six gun-boats. The convoy came to an anchor about four, nearly six miles N. W. of *Ensenada*, which is distant from *Buenos Ayres* about thirty-two miles, lower down the river. The next day the gun-boats each took in an eighteen pounder at the bow, and drew in towards the shore with the smaller armed vessels, about two miles and a half above *Ensenada* : the light brigade having been embarked in vessels of light tonnage, they also closed in to the shore, and by twelve o'clock the preparations announced an early landing. Accordingly, orders were issued

to the different troops to be in readiness to dis-
embark the next morning, each soldier to be
provided with three days provision, ready dressed,
and a like quantity of liquor: the latter part of
this order was verbally communicated, and does
not appear to have been general, as the Rifle
Corps and others never received it, and, consequently, depending upon the supplies on shore
through the usual departments, were left to provide for themselves: there is no doubt but it was
a mistake; but where *orders are regularly communicated in writing, and properly distributed
to troops,* such serious mistakes are not so likely
to arise.

The disembarkation commenced at day-light,
on Sunday, the 28th of June, without the least
opposition, and our glasses gave no appearance
of an enemy in any part of the country, of which
we had a very extensive view. General Craufurd's
was the first brigade which landed; and as a bar
of sand prevented the approach of the flats to
the shore, the men were obliged to wade some
distance: a passage, however, having been found
through this bar, the remainder of the troops
landed perfectly dry at the mouth of a small
rivulet, which being the only spot admitting the
approach of boats, it was dark before the whole

R

of the troops could be got on shore; two light three-pounders were also landed. The light brigade and Sir Samuel Auchmuty's pushed on to a ridge about four miles advanced in the country; but which they were obliged to gain by a circuitous route through *Ensenada,* so as to avoid an extensive morass, covering nearly the whole space between the sea and the rising ground. Brigadier-General Lumley's, and part of Colonel Mahon's, occupied the huts of *Ensenada,* and some detached ones in the neighbourhood. About one mile between the landing-place and the village was an enclosed battery, but which had been dismantled and abandoned, as well as two or three ships lying close to the shore : the huts had also been forsaken by their inhabitants. Some horses were procured here, which served to mount a few dragoons, the staff officers, and *their servants ;* but *none* could be obtained for the field officers of regiments. The three-pounders were drawn by thirty-six seamen, who attended the whole march for this purpose. We were joined at this place by an Anglo-American, who served us as a guide on the march to *Buenos Ayres.* This man had resided for many years in the neighbourhood of the town, where he had some property, and a family. Expecting great advantages from his

betraying the government that had so long
protected him, he took the earliest opportunity of
joining the invading army, with which he was, of
course, obliged to evacuate the country likewise.

On Monday morning, at eight, we moved by
the left to pass the swamp between us and the
light brigade. It was not possible to get through
it with a greater front than one section, or to
march in more than a single column, the head of
which had not cleared it before one in the afternoon: for two miles and a half, we were constantly
up to our knees in mud and water. On this ridge
we found Sir Samuel Auchmuty's brigade only,
General Craufurd having pushed on with his,
several miles in advance: here Colonel Mahon's
joined Sir Samuel's, and passed the night, General
Lumley's only advancing about two miles further,
after leaving his dismounted dragoons with the
main body. The 36th passed the night in advance
of the 88th. The troops were without cover for
the night, which was favorable enough, and the
railing forming the enclosures for cattle in the
neighbourhood of some huts, amply supplied fuel.
General Lumley having taken the precaution of
bringing from *Monte Video* several of the country
people accustomed to catching cattle, his brigade
was always well supplied with fresh meat; for,

though the natives had driven their herds from our line of march, yet there remained more than necessary to supply the wants in this article: several flocks of sheep also came in our way, and some spirits were drawn along by fatigue parties, as we had no other mode of conveyance. This day the 38th and 87th Regiments, after many hours labour, dragged two light six-pounders through the marsh.

The next morning the brigade united, about eleven. This day's march was crossed by several streams and swampy spots. After advancing about nine miles, a halt was made in detached parties, without any view to regular formation, as the light troops had pretty well examined the country, and we always commanded an extensive range, which shewed us nothing but a few scattered horsemen, apparently unarmed, who kept hovering about us. Some skirmishing in the course of the day did not extend beyond a few shots from the advanced parties. Our position was about seven or eight miles from the river, which was intercepted from us by very flat and marshy grounds. No communication was kept up with the fleet, which had moved upwards towards *Buenos Ayres*.

On Wednesday, the 1st of July, the army closed,

and moved onwards with more order and regularity, as it was expected to have the ground we were approaching somewhat disputed. Our march was in three divisions, but on the same road. The light brigade led, with the two three-pounders: it was followed, at about one mile and a half, by General Lumley's, with the two six-pounders, and the main body, under General Whitelocke, brought up the rear. The right flank of this line of march was perfectly protected by the aforementioned morass, and the left covered by the Rifle Corps. Our only apprehensions were for such men as should drop out of the line of march through fatigue, or some other cause, as the country people hovered round, and were sure of cutting off such stragglers: we lost two or three by the dexterity of these fellows. We were much annoyed in our march by several streams with soft muddy bottoms, and some morassy spots; and had these been disputed by a spirited enemy, we should have encountered no small loss and difficulty in forcing them, as we could form but a very narrow front over these places. About two o'clock, the men were ordered to throw away their blankets, that they might proceed with greater alacrity to the village of *Reduction*, which it was intended to reach this day, and the possession of which it was supposed would be disputed. This village is about seven miles from *Buenos Ayres*, and two from the bank of the river: it consists of a church, and some detached houses of inferior description; but it possesses a good natural position for defence. As it was approached by the light brigade, only a small body of horsemen appeared, who were dispersed by one shot from our field pieces, and the ground was gained without opposition, the enemy having entirely evacuated it, concentrating their strength on the west side of the small river *Chieulo,* which flows under the town of *Buenos Ayres.* We now got sight of this capital; and the spirits of the troops were not a little cheered by a first view of the object which they expected to reward them most amply for all their toils and a tedious march. The advanced brigades pushed on to a position two miles beyond the village, which latter was occupied by General Whitelocke. with the remainder of the army. Some few of the enemy approached our piquets, during the night, and created a false alarm or two; but no other attempts were made to molest us. The troops, however, enjoyed but little repose, as it rained excessively, accompanied with thunder and lightning: we could not but regret this circumstance, as the men required some rest after a fatiguing and uncomfortable march; and that of the next day promised to be no less so. We could plainly discern the fires of the Spaniards under the town, which, added to those of some ships burning in the river, to prevent them falling into our hands, produced a fine effect. We supposed one large blaze under the town to proceed from the bridge; but this they never attempted to destroy.

CHAPTER IV.

Passage over the Chieulo.—*Action of the Evening of the 2d July.—Transactions during the 3d and 4th.*

At sunrise on the 2d July we were under arms, and an order was issued for those men, who could not undergo a fatiguing march, to fall out and join the rear guard: few, however, came within this description, and we proceeded on our route, wheeling to the left, and presenting our right flank to the river *Chieulo*, so as to ascend it as far as the pass of *Chico*, about five miles from its mouth. We continued in this direction for about the same distance through some marshy ground and over several streams, when a body of horse formed as if to oppose the head of our column. This corps consisted of about six hundred, and was supported on its right by a small wood, and on the left by some marshy grounds. The light brigade immediately formed into line, covered on its right by General Lumley's, which remained in open column ready to form *en potence :* the Rifle

Corps filed to the left to clear the wood and obtain possession, which having been effected, our light pieces began to play on the enemy, who dispersed after two or three rounds, and we continued our march without further molestation. We now inclined to the right, and about half past three o'clock arrived on the banks of the *Chieulo*, at the ford of *Chico*. There was no enemy opposite, and it was instantly forded, being about four feet deep, and thirty yards over: its current was not rapid, and the bottom was a firm gravel. The ammunition waggon belonging to our three pounders was carried over on men's shoulders; and the passage having been completely effected by these two brigades, over the obstacle we expected to have proved the most formidable on our march, they advanced towards the ridge, at the northern extremity of which *Buenos Ayres* is situated: this ridge was about two miles from this part of the river, and on it, it was supposed, we should take our position for the night. Our eyes were anxiously directed over the extensive plain we had passed, in expectation of seeing the main body of the army following us under General Whitelocke; but to our mortification there was not the least appearance of troops in our rear, a circumstance rather extraordinary to us, as his

S

distance from our column, on commencing the march, was scarcely two miles. We soon gained the foot of the rising ground, and the riflemen and some of the light brigade began to scour the thick hedges, and other cover afforded to the enemy, by the gardens and orange groves occupying the whole of the ridge. General Craufurd and Lumley's brigades had to advance in sections up a narrow and broken road; and when the former had attained the summit, he wheeled to the left, to attain a favorable position that had been mentioned to him: the firing was now pretty sharp in the advance; but the enemy's piquets were soon driven in by the rapid movements of this column. No symptoms of an enemy now appeared; the parties covering the head of the light brigade were called in, and it arrived, a few minutes after, at the angle of an open space, up which it was to move by wheeling to the right; a momentary halt was called to wait for the field pieces, that were at some distance in the rear; and many of the men leaned up against a house, for a little ease. Not a Spaniard was in view; but their neighbourhood was soon announced by a sudden discharge of grape and round shot from guns in several parts of the open ground. Surprized at this unexpected attack, the men shrunk for a moment, and the General himself felt a momentary hesitation; but as instantaneously recollecting himself, he ordered a general charge upon the enemy. Not an instant was lost in obeying this order, and with three cheers our brave fellows, advancing smartly in the form of a crescent, nearly surrounded the enemy's guns, which were soon abandoned by the Spaniards, who, dismayed at this movement, fled in every direction: those lining the hedges dispersed with the others, on seeing their artillery in our possession, amounting to ten brass field pieces of four and eight pounders, with one five and a half inch howitzer, few of which they had an opportunity of spiking. Many of the flying enemy were bayoneted, and General Craufurd continued the pursuit with his brigade, until he reached the heads of some of the streets of *Buenos Ayres,* where he formed, in expectation of General Gower, who was behind with Lumley's brigade. The loss on our part, at this gallant affair, was trifling, as the enemy's artillery was directed over the heads of our men.

The light brigade had moved on so briskly, after attaining the ridge, that the other, which was close at its heels at the time, did not keep up with it. General Gower was, therefore, at a loss to follow,

and made repeated enquiries after the light
brigade, whose position was at last pointed out
by an officer of the Rifle Corps, as well as by the
sound of the cannon and musketry it had been
engaged with. He pushed on towards the town,
and it was long after dark before he came up to
the ground occupied by the light brigade. General
Lumley's formed at the head of the streets opposed
to us, with its right thrown back, to cover that flank
from a wood to which it was exposed : the light
brigade was in a second line; and we were momentarily expecting the order to advance into the town,
particularly as some companies had been detached
on the flanks, with an apparent view of covering
such a movement. This General Craufurd had
already proposed doing; but General Gower
would not authorize the attempt, which, by all the
information we afterwards received, would have
been crowned with success, with but little if any
loss. Our vexation, when ordered to retire, may
therefore be easily conceived, and we gained, in
silence, the ground where the light troops had so
gallantly overthrown the first regular body of the
enemy that had dared to oppose our progress, and
which was about one mile and a half from the
skirts of the town. Here we lay on our arms,
having our piquets at the heads of the streets:

the night was a dreadful one to the troops, who were drenched in rain, and overpowered with fatigue and hunger, not having partaken of any refreshment for the last twelve hours : it was, however, borne with patience, the mens' spirits having been much raised by the success of the evening, and the expectation of crowning their wishes early in the morning by entering *Buenos Ayres.* No signs appeared of the main body with General Whitelocke, though reconnoitring parties had been detached in search of him.

Upon examination of the prisoners that had fallen into our hands this evening, it appeared that the whole Spanish force, amounting to about nine thousand men, had expected us at the bridge over the *Chiculo* close under the town, where they had strongly intrenched themselves, and brought together above fifty pieces of cannon, with a determination of defending this pass to the last moment. On learning that we were avoiding the bridge, they dispatched about six thousand men, in two columns; one to check us at a ford between the bridge and *Chico;* the second to move along the heights, and observe our motions above this pass. Having found that we had gained the western side of the *Chieulo,* the first mentioned column was ordered to retire, and occupy the position where it was put to the rout by the light brigade. The other column, afraid of being cut off from the town, took a circuitous route, and gained, at a late hour, *El Retiro:* those who had remained at the bridge were called in, with what cannon they could bring, having spiked and destroyed the remainder. General Linier was in person with the routed division, and we were afterwards informed, by one of his aid-de-camps, that he had been obliged to pass a great part of the night within our line of sentries, his retreat having been intercepted by the brisk advance of our troops.

Parties were detached early in the morning to search the adjoining houses for bread, liquor, and arms: these parties brought in many prisoners, who were found in the houses, after throwing off their uniforms, and concealing their arms. In the mean time, an officer of General Lumley's staff was dispatched into the town with a flag of truce, by General Gower. He was the bearer of a verbal summons to the Spanish General, requiring the surrender of the place to His Britannic Majesty's arms: in reply, Linier, who had escaped into the town before day-light, said that he could hold no communication with our General, but in writing. Accordingly Brigade-Major Roach was sent in a second time, carrying in writing the summons he had before verbally conveyed : **to** this the Spaniards refused to listen: and the return of the flag announced the advance of the enemy from the town to attack us in our position, and that the men composing these columns were in a state of intoxication. In consequence of this intelligence the advanced posts were reinforced, and the troops formed in the best order for applying the bayonet in case the Spaniards should approach within sufficient distance to allow us the use of it. Our piquets retired by degrees, as the enemy forced in upon them in an extended line, under cover of the hedges and gardens: they did not appear, however, in any compact body; and after keeping up this skirmishing for above two hours, they again retired into the town. There was some loss on our part in this affair, and the Spaniards suffered much from the fire of our riflemen, as appeared by the numbers who lay dead or wounded in every enclosure. It was always difficult to ascertain their loss, as they succeeded in bearing off many of the latter, and even some of the dead.

While we were expecting the enemy in our position, General Whitelocke made his appearance, with Sir Samuel Auchmuty's brigade, and the 45th, belonging to Colonel Mahon's, this officer remaining at *Reduction*, with several detachments of the regiment in the advance, and the dismounted dragoons of his brigade. It appeared that General Whitelocke had left his ground on the 2d, a very short time after we had moved from ours; instead of pursuing the same route with ourselves, he inclined to his left, and kept the high grounds, which led him many miles above the pass of *Chico*, thus rendering it impossible for him to join General Gower that evening, and he took up his position for the night about ten miles from us. He there received the intelligence of the proceedings of the former day, and joined us about two in the afternoon, on Friday, the 3d. Sir Samuel formed on our left, and, after waiting in this position until the Spaniards had totally disappeared, we were marched to different quarters in the neighbourhood, where the men were placed under cover. Our advanced posts occupied the same ground as on the former night.

On the 4th the troops took up their position of the 3d, and the same skirmishing took place as on that day. The Rifle Corps having expended their ammunition, General Lumley's brigade was ordered to relieve them about noon; they occupied the rear of the houses and orchards on the borders of the town, where the fire continued very hot for above two hours, during which time the Spaniards succeeded in forcing in the posts on the left, occupied by the 36th Infantry; by which movement they took the 88th, on that flank, and in reserve, whence this regiment was severely galled, until the enemy was dislodged by the fire of a six-pounder, which was brought up against the cover they occupied, and which forced them to retire. This firing ceased about four o'clock, and at dusk the Carabineers and 9th Light Dragoons, who had come up from *Reduction* this day, took the advanced duties for the night, those whom they relieved occupying their former quarters. The troops engaged this day had many officers wounded, and several men were left dead on the field, and numbers were brought in wounded.

The object of this day's operations was not very obvious to the army. We lost many men by occupying an advanced position during the day, which afforded a covered approach to the Spaniards, who, at pleasure, could come from the interior of the town, to insult these piquets. By retiring the advanced posts one or two hundred yards more to the rear, an open space between them and the skirts of the town gave a full view of the approach of such as should dare to quit the

T

streets. It was always easy to occupy the disputed ground at night, if necessary, as the Spaniards regularly concentrated their whole force within the precincts of the Castle, as soon as it became dusk, and the occupation of this ground could only become necessary, when it had been determined to push the columns into the town, which would thus enter the heads of the streets without molestation.

It would appear as if it had been at one time the intention of our leaders to attack the town this day; and as much had been intimated by General Craufurd to his brigade; but this intention was afterwards changed, and the assault put off to the next morning. In the evening a communication to this effect was made to the officers commanding regiments, and something of a plan of attack shewn them; but their instructions were very confined, and few explanations of the subject given them. In a *circular letter* addressed to officers commanding brigades, dated on the 4th of July, the Commander in Chief informs them that the Spaniards had refused to listen to any terms of surrender; and that the uncomfortable state of the army rendered it necessary for him to order a mode of attack, which, under other circumstances, he would have avoided, as the

purchase of the town at present must, unquestion-
ably, be at a greater price of blood than if he
were allowed, by a different season of the year,
and a different state of the troops, to proceed
against the place on another plan. In this same
letter, he likewise recommends it to the officers
to impress on the minds of those under their
immediate command the necessity of desisting
from violence towards unarmed men, women and
children. It will be necessary to add that this
circular letter was never inserted in public orders,
that it was never communicated to the troops in
any shape, nor were the observations respecting
unarmed men, women and children ever acted
upon; for it is not to be supposed that field
officers leading columns the next day, would
have recommended to their soldiers *to make no
prisoners,* had they known that such a letter as
above quoted, had been in existence. It was only
after the return of the army to *Monte Video* that
this letter was seen by a few officers, a copy of
which was forwarded, by General Whitelocke, to
be shewn to General Linier: the reader will
draw a particular inference from these circumstances.

It will be necessary before proceeding to narrate
the movements of the different columns on the

5th, to give a brief description of *Buenos Ayres*, which may assist the reader in forming an idea of the operations of this day, so disastrous to the British arms.

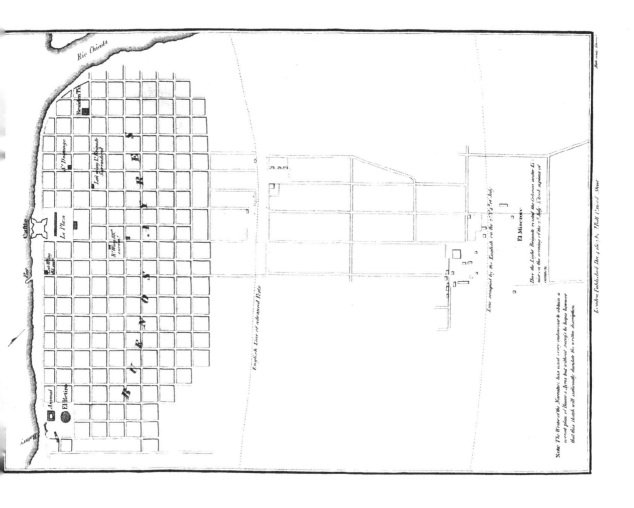

Rio Chiata

Castle

Res.dʳ Tʳˢ

Sᵗ Domingo

Los dos El Deposito Reprodʳ

La Plaza

Bʳᵗ Wharf &c occupied

Fort of the English

El Retiro

Arsenal

B U E N O S   A Y R E S

English Line of advanced Posts

Line occupied by the English on the 5ᵗʰ 6ᵗʰ & 7ᵗʰ July

El Miserere

Here the Light Brigade received the fire from under Liniers in the evening of the 5 Aug. S Yeok separate at corners.

Note: The Writer of the Narrative has used every endeavour to obtain a correct plan of Buenos Ayres but without success; he hopes however that this sketch will sufficiently elucidate the written description.

London Published Dec.r 1.1808, by I. Booth Duke Street

CHAPTER V.

Description of Buenos Ayres, *and Account of the Preparations made for its Defence.*

Buenos Ayres, the capital of the vice-royalty of *Paraguay,,* is built on the *Rio de la Plata :* it is bounded on the east side by a small river, called the *Chieulo,* over which is a wooden bridge communicating with the country, and is open all round. Like the description already given of *Monte Video,* its streets are rectangular, forming lots above one hundred paces square. The northern and western sides are bounded with gardens and orange groves, enclosed with strong hedges of the aloes and prickly pear, which grow here to a most luxuriant size; but few of the enclosures are of brick. In the centre of the town, on the face next the river, is situated the Castle, a square work, about one hundred paces on the exterior polygon, and flanked with small bastions: the walls are about fifteen feet high from the level of the interior to the top of the parapet, which is not raised above four feet from the rampart, the guns

being placed *en barbettee* on field carriages: it
has a ditch on the face next the town only, over
which is a draw-bridge. In this fortress (if it
can be considered worthy the appellation) is the
residence of the Governor, and it is likewise
occupied with other spacious buildings. The
Great Square, or as the Spaniards call it, by way
of distinctive excellency, *La Plaza*, separates the
Castle from the town, and it may be about two
hundred paces on the faces parallel with the river,
and about one hundred more on those perpendicular to it. An embellished arcade, with a
parapet over its capital, divides the square into
two parts, and from the angles proceed streets in
rectangular directions, excepting on its eastern
side, where only one street runs to the southward
and none eastward: the south face contains a
large church, with a lofty dome and parapet. All
the houses in this neighbourhood are lofty, and
surrounded with parapets above four feet high,
which circumstances give those in possession of
the faces of this square an entire command over
the Castle, and which proved the cause of General
Beresford's surrender in August, 1806. At
the north-west angle of the town, and close to
the river, is another extensive opening, called
La Plaza del Tauros, in which is erected *El*

Retiro, the amphitheatre for the exhibition of bull-fights. This building has twelve faces, of about ninety feet each on the outer side, and with six arched openings, about fourteen feet from the ground to their basement. The external walls are of brick; the interior divisions of wood, painted and embellished in an appropriate manner. The seats run round the area in which the bulls are engaged; six rows are uncovered; above, there is a row of boxes, and a corridor runs round the whole building. In the neighbourhood, and towards the river, are other larger buildings of brick, serving as the chief depot for the military stores and ordnance of *Buenos Ayres.* Various roads and streets lead into the *Plaza del Tauros,* but all at right angles with each other. Under the ridge near the river had been constructed this year, an enclosed battery flanking the approach in this direction, as there is a low unoccupied space, about one hundred yards wide, between the town and the river. *El Retiro* may be about one thousand yards from the Castle.

To the eastward of the *Great Square,* and one street above it, is another open space, where are barracks, and nearly opposite these the church and monastery of St. Domingo, the principal one in *Buenos Ayres* after the Cathedral. A very extensive building which had been originally intended as a royal hospital, and called *Residentia*, is situated at the east end of the town, over which are scattered other churches and squares of inferior note. The breadth of the city is about one mile, and its length two; the ground rising gradually from the river to its southern boundary, so as to place the whole of the buildings under the command of those occupying this ridge, as well as of those in possession of *El Retiro*, which over-looks the whole town to the castle.

At the time of our landing at *Ensenada*, few preparations had been made for immediately defending the interior of the town, and neighbourhood of the Castle, with the exception of provisioning the houses intended to be defended, and also providing in each the means of barricading the doors and windows. The enemy placed their chief dependence on being able to prevent the passage of our army over the *Chieulo*, and had accordingly strengthened their position on the bank next the town, and under the bridge. Here they had assembled the whole of their force in any state of discipline, as well as the whole of their transportable artillery, amounting to fifty-two pieces of large calibre. Finding it not to be the intention of our generals to force a passage at this spot (and which truly would have been a difficult task, as we had been obliged to leave our heavy artillery in the marshes), they dispatched two thirds of their number to check us higher up, and watch our movements after crossing the river at *Chico;* the remainder kept in their old position. It has already been seen how one of their columns was defeated and put to flight, by our light brigade the same evening, and that the second had been obliged to fall back, and occupy *El Retiro.* The dispersed division brought confusion and dismay into the town : it was now dark, and the victorious columns formed at the head of the streets, which the Spaniards expected to have been immediately entered. Their leader was missing, without being able to account for his absence; and, in this state of terror and disorder, the inhabitants only prepared to receive us as their conquerors : they threw off their uniforms and their arms, waiting in momentary expectation of seeing our troops march in. Instead of this movement, they were astonished at our making a retrogade one : they had time to recollect themselves, and their chief officers ordered in the division from the bridge, with what cannon they could draw, leaving the remainder in a useless state : this ordnance was placed in the square, at

U

the debouché of the streets leading from the ground we had taken up; and the like was done at the *Plaza del Tauros,* where their best troops were disposed of, knowing that this spot, once in the possession of our troops, the town became completely under our command. Trenches were cut in the principal streets near the *Great Square,* and cannon placed to flank them : other pieces were mounted on the Citadel, to cover the approach by the river. General Linier having found means of re-entering the town, immediately adopted measures to restore confidence to its inhabitants; and well knowing the effects of a superstitious zeal over minds which will not even feel more noble motives of action, he employed the clergy in support of these measures. The Bishop exhausted all the rhetoric and powers of religious oratory to an immense congregation, collected on the morning of the 3d at *El Retiro,* and succeeded by holy promises to make those resume their arms who had come to a former determination of laying them down, and induced many others to bear them, who could not hitherto be prevailed upon. Even women felt a sort of inspiration on the occasion, and several took an active part, by lighting and casting grenadoes from the tops of the houses, as the British columns passed under : one was killed in man's uniform. A great part of the slaves, whom it had not been deemed safe as yet to trust with arms, were provided with weapons of defence, and these were chiefly a rough sort of pike, composed of blades of knives attached to canes about fourteen feet long. The number thus employed in defending the interior parts of *Buenos Ayres* consisted of about nine thousand regulars, militia, and volunteer corps, in some state of discipline, and six thousand in irregularly formed companies. Of these troops, five thousand occupied the houses, in which they were barricaded and provisioned, being their best shots, and having ample supplies of ammunition: two thousand occupied *El Retiro* and its neighbourhood : the others were distributed in the Castle, and employed as occasion should demand. It is, however, necessary to observe, that in this enumeration of the Spanish force employed in the defence of this town, it was difficult to establish it on any regular data ; for even the Spaniards themselves had no certain means of collecting returns of men who took up arms and lay them down at pleasure : the above enumeration appears, nevertheless, to approach as near the truth as can be expected under such circumstances, and was formed by accounts from various sources, and compared together.

Among other precautions, that of illuminating the town, during the night, was not neglected; but the additional lamps, used for this purpose, were composed of clay, and being placed on the outside of the houses, might have been easily extinguished : in the more important points, barrels of pitch were fired. The measures, thus adopted for defence, had not effect the first night we took up our position at the *Miserere;* but no time was lost in the interval between our arrival and assault, to complete them.

It was in the face of such preparations, made by a people who appeared fully determined to lose none of the advantages to be derived from the leizure we had given them, that four thousand five hundred British soldiers, at the utmost, were ordered to enter the town, by force, on the morning of Sunday, the 5th of July. The troops were under arms about four o'clock in the morning; but, owing to various delays, it was day-light before the different columns were formed at the heads of the streets through which they were to penetrate into the town. Their disposition was as follows.

CHAPTER VI.

Assault of Buenos Ayres, *on the 5th July.*

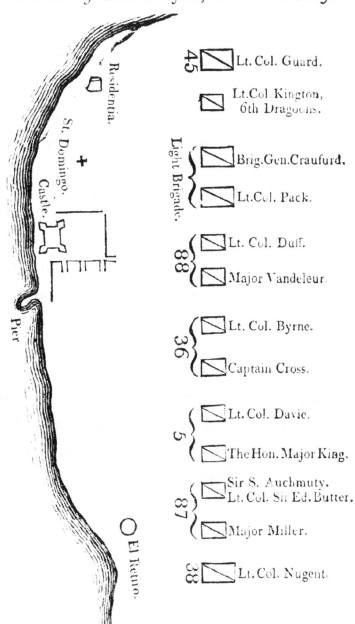

The 45th Infantry were directed against *Resi-dentia*, where they were to lodge themselves. General Craufurd was likewise to pierce to the church of St. Domingo, and take possession, as also of the neighbouring houses, in conjunction with Lieutenant-Colonel Pack, who led the left wing of the light brigade, which brought its two three-pounders into the town, along with it. The other columns were to pierce to the river, but what they were to do when there, depended on the further instructions they were to receive, for they were provided with none beyond that point. The 87th were directed to move down the two streets to the right of *El Retiro*, and the 38th in single column, was to attack this building after turning the left of the town. None of the columns were made acquainted with the means of communicating with each other, nor on what points a retreat was to be effected in case resistance should be found too powerful to penetrate through the town. In short, most of the officers were as deficient in the necessary instructions for conducting their divisions as they were ignorant of the plans of their chiefs. The columns had been ordered to take in some of their intrenching tools with them, but these were little qualified to force the obstacles we had to encounter.

The troops were all anxious to move forward, while darkness, in some degree, veiled their advance; but the sun was rising ere some field pieces in the centre gave the signal to commence the attack, and at this moment the columns were put in motion. Their operations were not all of equal interest, and particular notice only will be taken of those whose situations affected the fate of the army on this occasion.

To commence on the right, the 45th Infantry obtained possession of *Residentia*, after meeting with some opposition from a body of Spaniards stationed, with artillery, in an open space. The guns were soon abandoned, and there being no resistance from the houses in the neighbourhood, this extensive building was soon crowned with the colours of the regiment. But little loss was encountered in this affair; after which, Lieutenant-Colonel Guard marched at the head of his grena-diers, to pierce through the streets separating him from the light brigade: in his progress, a piece of ordnance was brought against him, and which killed or wounded about ten or twelve men. He soon got possession of this gun, and continued his march to the church of St. Domingo, where he was taken, with General Craufurd. The Spaniards made repeated attempts to recover *Residentia*

after Colonel Guard's departure, but Major
Nicholls had so well disposed of part of his
men on the top of the buildings, and sallied out
so opportunely with others, that he constantly
repulsed them, and took four of their cannon.
The British colours remained flying on *Residentia*
until evacuated by the 45th, after the termination
of the negotiation.

The Carabineers, who had the piquet duty
during the night, advanced with the other
columns, and entered the town, which they
penetrated to some distance, with the loss of
several men. Colonel Kington, who led them,
having received a severe wound in the leg, and
Captain Burrell being killed, they were forced to
retire; but left their commander in the hands of
the enemy.

The right wing of the light brigade, preceded
by an advanced guard of one subaltern and thirty
men, moved down the street on the right of
the church of St. Domingo. It received the
fire of several guns on its left flank, but not
sufficient opposition to arrest its progress to the
banks of the river. Here, on turning to its left,
it entered an open space, in which it became
dreadfully exposed to the fire of musketry from
the neighbouring houses : above one half of the

advanced party were stretched on the ground, and among its wounded, the officer commanding it. The fire thickened upon the column, and a movement to the rear was deemed adviseable; but, before undertaken, the wounded men were collected under the shelter of a wall, whence they were afterwards removed into the church, which now became the object of attack. Above half an hour elapsed before an entrance could be forced, which was effected by discharging a field piece through the doors. The colours of the 71st Regiment were found decorating the inside of the building; they were instantly taken down, and the Rifle Corps, and others of the column, forcing their way to the parapets, displayed it on them. The Spaniards who were on the top of the building retired to the summit of the dome, drawing after them the only ladder by which they could be got at. The Spaniards, aware of the importance of this post, advanced several strong corps against it, and with cannon: our own three-pounder could be but badly served, as the men found it impossible to work it under the heavy fire from the houses, which were momentarily reinforced with men and ammunition; the Spaniards likewise succeeded in enfilading the different openings of the church, which obliged our men to seek for shelter under

X

the walls. To make a sortie, with any chance of success, was impossible, as was proved by several attempts, in one of which the brave and accomplished soldier Major Trotter was killed, being pierced with several balls: his loss damped the spirits of the party in no slight degree. A summons was now made to General Craufurd to lay down his arms, or that the church should be battered about his ears. He refused; and the enemy instantly commenced carrying their threat into execution: the church soon felt the effects of this cannonade; and, it being impossible to silence or answer it, General Craufurd, after consulting with the field officers of his wing, surrendered, about two o'clock in the afternoon.

Lieutenant-Colonel Pack, with the left wing of this brigade, moved, with an advanced guard of equal strength with the former, and pierced, but with great loss, to some buildings to the left of St. Domingo. He here lodged his party, and did much execution with his riflemen from the tops of these houses. Colonel Pack, knowing that General Craufurd was in the church, proceeded thither singly, to consult with him about further operations; but the enemy having cut off the communication between the two wings, he found it impossible to rejoin his, and was obliged to share the fate of General Craufurd. Lieutenant-Colonel Cadogan remained in command of the left wing, which was now much pressed by reinforcements to their opponents ; and, after expending nearly their whole ammunition, a parley took place between them and the Spaniards. In this interval, the latter crowded towards the occupied houses, which occasioned a discharge from some of our men, by which an aid-de-camp of Linier's was severely wounded. The Spaniards instantly abandoned the spot, and our men took this opportunity of evacuating their present post and occupying another, which, however, did not prove so defensible. Here they remained until necessity obliged them to become prisoners of war, about half an hour before their right wing lay down their arms.

Lieutenant-Colonel Duff, of the 88th, had been ordered, by Brigadier-General Lumley, to proceed, with the right wing of his regiment, as far as he could without too great a sacrifice, and to endeavour to obtain possession of a church on his right. About fifty yards before reaching this building, the fire opened from the tops of the houses on his left. The column pushed on, and gained the church, in front of which was a court, the gate of which being open, our troops entered it; but the doors of the church resisted every effort to break them. During this time, about thirty men had fallen by the excessive fire from the surrounding houses, and this post was therefore evacuated. The column pushed on through a heavy discharge of musketry, as far as within a hundred paces of the south-west angle of the *Great Square*, when it became impracticable to penetrate farther: about one third of the column had now fallen, and Lieutenant-Colonel Duff ordered it to turn to the left, where it forced open and entered three houses which had not been occupied by the enemy, but which were completely commanded by them from those adjoining. Our men were placed at the doors and windows, whence they were driven by a hail of musket balls from a numerous enemy, who encreased every moment. The apertures of the houses were now shot into from the opposite ones, and the men falling fast, the officers were reduced to surrender about noon.

The liberty will be taken of narrating the progress of the left column of this regiment, in the words of an officer who accompanied it on this occasion; particularly as it penetrated beyond the advance of the others, and shews more minutely the mode of defence employed by the Spaniards

in the neighbourhood of the *Great Square.* " At
" the signal of attack, the left wing of the 88th,
" led on by Major Vandeleur, advanced down
" the street of *St. Pedro,* being the second to the
" westward of the Castle; and as it had been
" particularly enjoined upon its commander to
" reach the river, he penetrated smartly through
" the town to attain this object. Not the least
" opposition appeared until we had got down
" about half the street, but the utmost silence
" reigned; even the dogs were tied up in the
" courts. Here we received some shots from
" the crossing streets, and on reaching the third
" crossing from the river, were flanked by some
" cannon placed between us and the square.
" The firing now opened from the tops of the
" houses, whence we also received grenadoes and
" earthen pots, filled with composition, which
." burnt several of our party; as the river was
" now opening to our view, we paid but little
" attention to these assailants. Two pieces of
" artillery were also discharged at the head of the
" column from the bottom of the street, after
" which they were withdrawn by the Spaniards
" towards the *Great Square.* We were exposed
" to heavy showers of grape and landgridge on
" our right flank, before we attained the last

" square of buildings which terminates the town
" on this side. Our men had fallen fast at the
" angles, and one officer had already become a
" victim to a species of firing it was out of our
" power to resist or oppose. In crossing the last
" street an obstacle presented itself, which re-
" quired our utmost exertions to surmount: this
" was a breast work, composed of bullocks' hides
" made into sacks, and filled with the earth from
" a ditch in front of it, about six feet deep and
" twelve wide. As we gained this intrenchment
" in the reverse, the parapet was soon scrambled
" over, and we sprung into the ditch, out of which
" we were obliged to assist each other. While
" thus situated, the fire was dreadfully hot upon
" us from the houses on both sides, and we lost
" numbers at this spot. The joy at thus gaining
" the point we were ordered to make was not
" little; but our disappointment may be con-
" ceived, when we found the street had no outlet
" at this end, but by a small ramp to the right,
" enfiladed by the Castle, which now opened upon
" us at a distance of about two hundred yards.
" Somewhat staggered at this unexpected situa-
" tion, we thought it proper to occupy a temporary
" lodgment, in hopes of being supported by, or
" communicating with the columns on our flanks,

" It was with difficulty we could burst the gateway
" of an enclosure about ten yards square, with
" one face open to the river, the others having a
" low range of buildings with a sloping roof,
" which was crowned at the crest with a parapet,
" behind which many Spaniards lay concealed.
" We left some men to guard the entrance, but
" the enemy soon cleared the gateway by their
" enfilading shots from the back of the low
" buildings under which our men were sheltered.
" It was impossible to get at them, and several
" attempts to ascend the roofs were found im-
" practicable. Those who escaped from the
" gateway entered, after violent efforts, an un-
" occupied house, from the top of which they
" expected to silence or answer their opponents.
" A field piece was brought to bear against this
" house from the angle near the breast-work, in
" the ditch of which Captain Chisholm had
" remained with his section, to secure the rear
" of the column against insults from that quarter:
" the sound of this field piece alone announced
" to him its approach, and forming a banquette
" with the dead bodies which filled the bottom of
" the ditch, he succeeded in directing his fire
" against the gun, which the Spaniards aban-
" doned. They however returned, and fired a

" second shot, and were again driven off by
" Captain Chisholm, who being now severely
" galled by the fire from the houses, became
" necessitated to shelter his men at the foot of
" the scarp of the work. The situation of the
" column was now alarming. No communica-
" tions could be maintained between its detached
" parties, as the fate of many shewed it to be
" certain death to quit their cover; to retreat
" was impracticable, and all hopes of support
" vanished, as the sound of firing receded from
" instead of approaching us. We remained in
" this state above two hours, when the enemy
" made attempts to pierce through the walls and
" roofs; half the division lay either dead or
" wounded, and one shell, or a few grenades,
" would have determined the fate of the remainder,
" whom the officers did not deem themselves
" authorized to sacrifice to no purpose: they
" accordingly hoisted a flag of truce, which the
" Spaniards attended to, and received this column
" as prisoners of war."

This regiment having been directed against the
Great Square, where the defence was concentrated, its loss was accordingly proportioned to
the opposition it met with. Four officers were
killed and twelve wounded: out of four hundred

and fifty-four rank and file led into the town, nearly one hundred were killed, and one hundred and twenty wounded.

The 36th's right wing, consisting of six companies, accompanied by Brigadier-General Lumley, and led by Lieutenant-Colonel Byrne, moved down the street of St. Nicholas : they met with the same kind of opposition as had been encountered by the columns on the right. On reaching the second street from the river, they suffered from a field piece and the tops of the houses. Some of these were occupied, and the left wing, having inclined to its right, here joined it. The General thought it adviseable to halt, and afterwards to retreat; but Colonel Byrne represented that it would be attended with very destructive effects, if attempted while exposed to be followed by the artillery then playing on them. The General then left it to Colonel Byrne, to act as he thought proper in this emergency, who immediately ordering his men to follow him, he charged, and obtained possession of the gun, which he spiked. The regiment remained in this neighbourhood for some hours; but a cry of " retreat " came from different quarters, and Colonel Byrne, much against his inclination, was obliged to adopt this measure, which he effected with scarcely any loss.

Y

The 5th penetrated to the river, with very little, if any opposition, where they posted themselves in different houses without the direction of the cannon from the citadel. The Spaniards drew two guns along the beach, and fired at the houses thus occupied by the 5th; but as their shots were ill directed, and at a long range, very little mischief was done.

It has already been observed, that the 87th were to pierce through the town by the two streets on the right of *El Retiro;* but, by some mistake, they were conducted through those directly leading on the *Plaza del Tauros.* Sir Samuel Auchmuty, with Lieutenant-Colonel Sir Edward Butler, headed the right wing, and it arrived near the debouché, when it became exposed to the heavy discharge of guns which enfiladed it, and which levelled the leading sections to the ground. To avoid this, the hedges were forced on the right, and the column, inclining to this direction, entered the next street, which led to the river. This they attained; but not without much loss from the guns which flanked them on the left. Having lodged themselves in a large house, the Spaniards from *El Retiro* attempted to drive them from it; but, as the intention of the enemy was now engaged by the 38th, these attempts were unsuccessful. The left wing of the 87th had to perform the same movement as the right before joining it, nor did it suffer less in so doing.

The 38th had in the mean time moved down to the left of *El Retiro*, and inclining to the right arrived at the north-west angle of the *Plaza del Tauros*, where the enemy's artillery opened against them. Here they halted, while a party of the regiment from the rear, filed round the grounds about the open space, and took possession of the battery of *Abascal*, whence they ascended, and took the artillery in flank, which opposed the advance of their regiment. These guns were immediately abandoned, and those working them fled into the neighbouring houses, where they fell victims to the fury of our soldiers.

The enemy's artillery was now turned upon themselves, and against the building, which contained a large body of their best troops, who kept up a smart fire of musketry through the arched openings. They were notwithstanding soon driven from these, and the 87th, who had reconnoitred the operations of the 38th, immediately joined them in the attack of *El Retiro*, and which now became so warm, that those within dreading the

Y 2

fate of their companions, who were bayoneted in the neighbouring houses, should they make any further resistance, immediately held out a white flag, and surrendered at discretion about half past eight o'clock. About eight hundred were made prisoners, the others having escaped into the town: twenty-nine pieces of artillery, including two mortars, fell into the hands of the 38th and 87th: and a quantity of military stores was found in the arsenal. The loss of the 87th was great on this occasion, both in officers and men, as they had been exposed to heavy and close discharges of pieces of large calibre, loaded with landgridge and grape.

At noon the firing had nearly ceased in all quarters, and the British troops remained in possession of the two posts, against which their efforts should have been alone directed at this period, namely, *El Retiro* and *Residentia*, which were both obtained at a trifling loss compared with what befel the army at the other attacks. Above seventy officers and one thousand men were killed, or badly wounded. One hundred and twenty officers and fifteen hundred rank and file were taken prisoners; and fifteen hundred stands of excellent arms fell into the hands of the

Spaniards; and nearly the whole of this loss was encountered at those points where there was no possibility of success, in the unconnected and unsupported manner in which these attacks were made.

CHAPTER VII.

Transactions in Consequence of the Issue of the Attack.—Observations thereon.

THE officers taken with the different divisions were marched, as they surrendered, to the Castle, where they were politely received by Generals Linier and Balbiani. It required the exertions of the Spanish gentlemen who escorted the British, to protect them from the insults of many of the rabble, several of whom even levelled their fire-arms at them. The privates were distributed into various prisons.

The officers in the Castle having signed their paroles, by which they bound themselves not to carry arms, directly or indirectly, against His Spanish Majesty, or his allies, during the war, or until regularly exchanged, we had refreshments brought us, and were disposed of in two large rooms looking westward over the parapet along the beach, and a strong guard, of their best looking grenadiers, placed over us, under the plea of protecting our persons.

Our fleet had been lying opposite to *Buenos Ayres* for some days, but entirely ignorant of our operations. The larger ships could not come within five or six miles of the shore. They knew by the firing, on the morning of the 5th, that we were pushing into the town; and on observing our colours flying on *El Retiro*, the smaller armed vessels drew close in and opened a communication, bringing on shore refreshments for the troops. General Whitelocke had removed his head quarters to the neighbourhood of *El Retiro;* and it would appear as if further operations against the town had been settled between the naval and military commanders, as orders were given to assist in landing some battering cannon, and the gun brigs took up a position, the next morning, under the pier, for bombarding the Castle and neighbourhood. About noon, on the 6th, the gun boats opened against the Castle, whence some heavy pieces were directed at them. This cannonading continued but half an hour, without doing much damage on either side, three or four shots only having struck the Castle, one of which dropped in the Spanish General's room.

This sudden stop put to the bombardment astonished us much, and appeared to have been the consequence, on the part of our General, of some communication made to him by a flag which

left the Castle a few minutes before the firing
commenced. The Spaniards appeared to dread
nothing so much as the bombarding of the town,
and it occasioned no little ferment among them.
It was said in our army, and on the authority of
our own generals, that a threat had been conveyed,
of making the English prisoners answer, with their
lives, any continuation of the bombardment; but
not a hint of this nature was ever dropped before
the English officers in the Castle, who were in
constant conversation with the Spanish aid-de-
camps, and other officers of high rank. Indeed,
their personal safety was pledged to them on the
strongest assurances, whatever might be the result
of any further proceedings between the armed
parties.

In the afternoon, Major-General Gower arrived
at the Castle, and opened a negotiation with
General Linier*; a cessation of hostilities was

---

* He returned again in the evening, and alarmed at General
Linier's expressing himself as unable to control the undisciplined
rabble in the town, he adopted the rash idea of evacuating the
post of *El Retiro*, the possession of which, at this time, alone
guaranteed the safety of the army. Orders were accordingly
given by him to this effect, but Sir Samuel Auchmuty, and
General Lumley, foreseeing the fatal consequences of such a
movement, opposed it with firmness; and, by this opposition,
prevented a measure which would have been attended with the
sacrifice of the remainder of the army.

agreed upon until the next day at noon, and the interval was to be employed in endeavours to bring about a final arrangement, which accordingly took place, on the following conditions:

A Definitive Treaty between the Generals in Chief of His Britannic Majesty and of His Catholic Majesty, as per the following Articles.

I. There shall be from this time a cessation of hostilities on both sides of the river *Plata.*

II. The troops of His Britannic Majesty shall retain, for the period of two months, the fortress and place of *Monte Video,* and, as a neutral country, there shall be considered a line drawn from *San Carlos* on the west, to *Pando* on the east; and there shall not be, on any part of that line, hostilities committed on any side, the neutrality being understood only that the individuals of both nations may live freely under their respective laws, the Spanish subjects being judged by theirs, as the English by those of their nation.

III. There shall be on both sides a mutual restitution of prisoners, including not only those which have been taken since the arrival of the

Z

troops under Lieutenant-General Whitelocke, but also all those His Britannic Majesty's subjects captured in *South America* since the commencement of the war.

IV. That for the promptest dispatch of the vessels and troops of His Britannic Majesty, there shall be no impediment thrown in the way of the supplies of provisions which may be requested for *Monte Video*.

V. A period of ten days, from this time, is given for the reimbarkation of His Britannic Majesty's troops to pass to the north side of the river *La Plata*, with the arms which may actually be in their power, stores, and equipage, at the most convenient points which may be selected, and during this time provisions may be sold to them.

VI. That at the time of the delivery of the place and fortress of *Monte Video*, which shall take place at the end of the two months fixed in the second article, the delivery will be made in the terms it was found, and with the artillery it had when it was taken.

VII. Three officers of rank shall be delivered for and until the fulfilment of the above articles by both parties, being well understood that His

Britannic Majesty's officers who háve been on their parole, cannot serve against *South America* until their arrival in *Europe*.

Done at the Fort of *Buenos Ayres*, the 7th day of July, 1807, signing two of one tenor.

JOHN WHITELOCKE,
Lieut.-Gen. Commanding.

GEORGE MURRAY,
Rear-Adm. Commanding.

SANTIAGO LINIERS.

CESAR BALBIANI.

BERNARDO VELASCOS.

Four months had been applied for by the British Commander for the evacuation of *South America,* but a longer term than two would not be granted. Endeavours were likewise made to open the port of *Buenos Ayres* for our English merchants at *Monte Video,* during the period allowed for the evacuation; but this was strongly resisted, on the ground of its being contrary to the laws of *Spain* for the government of her American colonies.

The detachment left at *Reduction* quitted it on the 6th, and advanced towards the bridge over the *Chieulo;* there were a few Spaniards on the town side, but no opposition was made to its progress over the river, which it crossed at a village above the bridge, excepting a small party which remained on the opposite side until the next day, when the whole joined.

On Wednesday, the 8th, the English officers were escorted from the Castle to *El Retiro.* On their way, along the beach, they beheld the melancholy spectacle of a heap of our brave fellows, who had fallen in the street of St. Pedro: they were stripped perfectly naked, and thrown together on this spot. The Spanish officers returned with all their countrymen in our possession; and in the afternoon many of our privates were brought in, and the whole exchange was effected the next day, excepting only such of our wounded as could not be removed with safety. The reimbarkation commenced immediately. This was done by means of the smaller vessels conveying the troops out to the transports, which could not approach within four or five miles of the shore: even the boats could not close within eighty yards, and the men were obliged to wade over a broken and rocky bottom to reach them. Many of the wounded were taken in at the pier. Several days elapsed before the reimbarkation was completed; in which interval, many desertions took place, owing to the temptations held out to our men;

but this circumstance having been communicated to General Linier, he gave up as many as could be secured, amounting to about thirty. Several escaped detection, and were left behind.

On the 13th, about noon, the fleet got under weigh, and anchored again for the night. The wind blowing favorably the next morning, from the N.W. it set sail once more, and arrived, about nine in the evening, at *Monte Video*, twenty-six days after it had left the same port to proceed against *Buenos Ayres*.

And thus terminated, so fatally for the British arms in *South America*, an expedition from which so much had been expected by the British nation, whose government had spared no expence in appointing and transporting an army calculated to ensure success, as far as it depended on pre-paratory measures to obtain it. The failure cannot be attributed to the want of that courage and per-severance which constitute the chief features in the character of the English soldier: regimental officers and men did their duty " *like brave, like* " *gallant soldiers*," to use the language of one of the generals: the list of killed and wounded will support this assertion ; but the greater part of the troops were employed by their leaders in a plan of attack where neither courage or intrepidity were of any avail; they were sent into situations where women and children who could pull a trigger were formidable enemies; they were instructed, on these occasions, nay, positively ordered, on pain of the severest punishments, not to fire a single shot, but to make use of the bayonet only, and against what? against brick walls, and houses strongly barricaded, while they remained exposed to showers of musketry over their heads. The despair of the men and officers could only be equalled by their indignation against those who had ordered them to a certain slaughter, without a chance of success. The defences prepared in the town, to meet the attack, could not have been unknown to those who planned it, as the information of all the prisoners who fell into our hands, after the 2d, corresponded on this subject. By some expressions which dropped from two briga- diers, it appeared that they had never been consulted in forming a plan of attack: it was merely shewn to Colonel Pack (who was tho- roughly acquainted with every avenue and approach to the Castle), after it had been decided on, and this officer gave his opinion strongly against it, and was known to declare that he foresaw it would have an unfortunate issue. He strongly recommended our gaining possession of *El Retiro* and *Residentia,* which we could afterwards maintain against any force that could be brought against us : we could then open a free communication with the fleet, to obtain from it stores and provisions, besides heavy ordnance to threaten the town, which would then lie completely at our mercy. A bombardment would either oblige the enemy to surrender or come out to meet us; in which case the issue could not be doubtful.

Our Commander in Chief declared that he was prevented, by his instructions, from bombarding the town, which, he said, principles of humanity also forbad. But let the reader decide upon the least cruel of the two methods, the one adopted, or that avoided on this occasion. By the former, a heated and enraged soldiery are ordered to storm the habitations of individuals, where the greatest exertions of officers cannot prevent the most cruel outrages towards men, women, and children, besides a general plunder of property. In a bombardment, some houses are damaged, and inhabitants killed, but the alarm occasioned is the greatest part of the mischief. The Spanish officers themselves declared, that a bombardment would have made the inhabitants yield up the place, for, against this mode of warfare, they had no other opposition to make than from a few guns without cover. Besides, whatever may have been the General's instructions, or however powerful his principles of humanity may prove at times, yet there is no doubt that he once forgot these, and preparations were commenced for firing on the town, but they as suddenly ceased. It would appear that the embarkation of mortars and shells at *Monte Video*, was merely intended to ballast the vessels conveying them to *Buenos Ayres*.

As our commanders were determined on entering the place, and carrying it at the point of the bayonet, why was it not done the same evening that the dispersion of three thousand of their best troops at the entrance of their streets threw confusion and dismay among the Spaniards in the town? If it was not deemed prudent to follow up this success at the moment, why was it not done the day after, or on the morning of the 4th? In our situation, an hour's delay was a serious sacrifice; to our opponents an important advantage. Were our leaders afraid of obtaining *Buenos Ayres* on too easy terms? Were they anxious of binding their brows with that laurel only which was plucked dripping with human blood? To a particular General, it was said, had been left the whole direction of the military operations; and, if so, he certainly appears to have been guided by that confidence in his own plans, which is more the effect of temerity and self-opinion, than the offspring of genius, or well established experience. These remarks on the measures adopted in carrying on this short campaign, and on the men with whom these measures originated, are not to be supposed as proceeding from a few individuals only: no, they were loud and general throughout the whole army, who were not very nice in venting a just indignation at having seen their hopes frustrated through *ignorance*, and, its inseparable companion, *presumption*, after undergoing for so long a period a tedious navigation, and a most fatiguing march. This indignation was the stronger when they reflected upon having been sent to meet dangers, by chiefs who thought these too great to expose themselves to any personal risk in sharing them. If it be asked, where were Generals Whitelocke and Gower, with their staff, when the army was sent into *Buenos Ayres?* the answer is, that they remained behind, just within sound of cannon; and that they did not stir from their quarters until about removing them, on the 6th, to the neighbourhood of *El Retiro*, after it had been well secured by the columns directed against it.

On the subject of the cessation of hostilities,

it may not be amiss to insert here an extract from a general order issued the day after the assault.

"G. O.   *Buenos Ayres,* 6th July, 1807.

"The Commander of the Forces, animated by the
" conduct of the troops under his command, and
" at the same time feeling for the distress of those
" in the hands of the enemy, has entered into a
" convention with the Spanish General, agreeing,
" that upon consideration of all British subjects
" taken before this period, as well as upon the late
" occasion, being liberated, he will desist from the
" operations against the town of *Buenos Ayres,*
" a measure dictated by humanity, and by a policy
" which, he trusts, will prove beneficial to *Great*
" *Britain.*"

A few observations on the above, arising from a knowledge of the circumstances, it is likewise hoped, will not be deemed impertinent. The gallantry of an army is certainly a most extraordinary plea for a General to assert as a motive for entering into a convention, by which the very object of his command is annulled. Had our troops been defeated at all points, instead of remaining in possession of the strongest posts of *Buenos Ayres;* had the soldiers remaining under his command, on the afternoon of the 5th, exhibited symptoms of cowardice, instead of a desire to follow up their success, what more could General Whitelocke have done to humiliate them, than to tie up their hands from further conquest, by a convention which not only sacrificed their future prospects, but even those advantages obtained to the country by the small army under Sir Samuel Auchmuty.

What is meant by his " *feeling for the distress " of those in the hands of the enemy*," it would be difficult to guess. Certainly, above one hundred officers, and about fifteen hundred men, had been nearly thirty-six hours in Spanish prisons; but, during this *long* period, no instance of distress, beyond the common fate of men taken in war, had fallen to their lot. The officers were detained in two large rooms in the Castle, and received as much attention as the peculiar circumstances under which General Linier and his officers were placed at the moment, would admit of. The men were kept in places of security, and the wounded received all the assistance it was possible to afford them. That a few insults were offered to some of the English prisoners cannot be denied; but the instances of kindness and good-will were far more numerous, and frequently borne testimony of by the prisoners after their release. Whatever insolence was shewn, came from the rabble; and the attentions we received were exhibited in every house. Perhaps our General judged of our situation by that of the Spaniards taken at *El Retiro*, who were promiscuously thrown together, without distinction between officers and privates; and when having been forty-eight hours without food, they remonstrated on the occasion, he desired the English officer who acted as interpreter, to tell them, in reply, that " they were damned rascals, " and that he would send them, in irons, on board " the ships." The English officer had too much philanthropy, as well as discretion, to interpret such language, particularly as he himself was a prisoner of war to the Spaniards, having come out with a flag of truce.

The plea of distress, which he wished the army to believe the English prisoners were suffering, was, therefore, unfounded; and his conduct to the Spaniards in his hands will shew, that his " feelings " were equally affected.

How a failure in an expensive expedition can be proved advantageous to the country fitting it out, will require the utmost ingenuity of the person advancing it. What renders this assertion the more extraordinary is, its proceeding from the

Commander of the expedition himself. Possibly the Ministers who appointed him to the command, foreseeing the *good* resulting from the loss of conquest, gave him instructions to this effect; if so, he cannot be accused of not having complied fully with them. Unless other stipulations can be shewn, than those appearing in the articles of the convention, it is certainly offering a gross insult to our understandings, to attempt to make us believe that any benefits have accrued to the English nation by the loss of their troops, treasures, and former conquests.

The attack of the 5th of July, and its consequences, have been melancholy subjects to dwell upon; and, before concluding them, a wish may be permitted to escape, that a public enquiry will shew upon whom the blame attaches on this occasion, and that ample justice will be done the nation, and the army employed in *Spanish America* in particular, by proving to them, that men in authority are not allowed to sport, at pleasure, with the lives and interests of those under their command, without feeling the weight of a just retribution.

CHAPTER VIII.

Some Account of the Country, and of the Manners and Customs of its Inhabitants.

A BRIEF description of the country, and a short account of such circumstances as came under our observation, in those parts we passed through, will prove more agreeable subjects.

On making Cape *St. Mary*, it appears high; but as it is approached, the mountainous parts recede, and a low land divides them from the sea. The small island of *Lobos*, or of *Seals*, bears about seven miles S.E. of *Maldonado*, and with the towers of this town, are excellent marks for ascertaining the north entrance of the river of *Plate*. The course from this to *Monte Video* is about W. by N. which steers clear of the *English Bank*, having a dangerous reef of rocks at its western extremity. The passage between this Bank and the island of *Flores* is about twelve miles; and it is adviseable to bring up at dusk, if near the island without seeing it, as it lies low, and the currents about it are not regular. The high land does not extend beyond the *Solis Mountains*, about twenty miles above *Maldonado;* beyond these, the ground is low and flat, and the hill of *Monte Video* is but a small one, not above one hundred and eighty feet high, which may be seen at the distance of about twenty-five miles, and is eighteen above *Flores*. The water of the *Rio de la Plata* is salt at *Monte Video*, and it is only fit for use about thirty miles higher up : it has a muddy appearance, but when allowed to settle, after being drawn up, it is clear and excellent. The river is very shallow, and admits of the passage, between the *Ortiz* and *Chica Banks*, in the way to *Buenos Ayres*, but of vessels drawing about fourteen feet: the depth is much affected by the winds, which swell the waters when blowing from the eastward, and *vice versa*. Not the least appearance of woods diversify the scene on the banks.

The land between *Ensenada* and *Buenos Ayres* for about four miles inward is not elevated above two feet from the level of the river, and consequently in the rainy season almost entirely under water. At the back of this marshy ground it gradually rises about twelve or fifteen feet higher, and presents pretty nearly the same level, until reaching the village of *Reduction:* it, however, has some inflections which receive the waters from the higher parts, and frequently present streams flowing towards the *Plata*. But a few wretched huts are seen scattered over this extent, affording shelter to the herdsmen who tend the immense droves of cattle, which here feed in the richest plains of clover. No signs of husbandry appear at the distance of a dozen miles in this direction from *Buenos Ayres*, with the exception of here and there some plantations of gourds.

Between *Reduction* and the capital is another wet level, which runs far up into the country, and through which the *Chieulo* winds, emptying itself into the *Plate*, after running for about two miles at the foot of the ridge upon which the city is built. This ridge rises to the height of about forty feet, and runs in a southerly direction, with some inflections: its ascent is gentle, and it presents a rich assemblage of groves and gardens bounded with hedges formed of the aloes and prickly pear. The fruit was on the trees when we arrived, in different stages of advancement, from the bud to the full grown and ripe orange and lemon: the apricot and peach trees were bare; but the gardens abounded with vegetables. The roads leading through these grounds we found deep and miry, but this may have arisen from the circumstances of the moment, as they had been much cut up by the great number of horses and carriages employed by the Spaniards in their military operations. The plantations extended as far as the eye could reach to the southward and westward of the town, some description of which has already been given to illustrate the attack of the 5th of July. Many of the houses are plaistered and white-washed, or otherwise coloured, particularly about the *Great Square*, which, with the embellishments of some pieces of ornamental architecture, serve to give it in this quarter a light and airy appearance. The domes and turrets with which the numerous churches are crowned, afford a relief to the town it does not possess by nature, but who has otherwise lavished on it advantages particularly favorable, were it in the hands of an industrious and cleanly people.

The inhabitants are mostly of Spanish origin, but a great number of other European descendants are found among them. Nothing could more strongly illustrate their indolence than a comparison of the interior of their houses with those of the Dutch at the *Cape*. In the Spanish houses, where the most common utensils are frequently of massy silver, the dirt and filth do not appear

B b

to have been removed from the floors for months, whereas among the inhabitants of the *Cape*, their cleanliness would lead a stranger to believe them possessed of far greater wealth than their much richer neighbours on the opposite coast. The Dutch are remarkable, likewise, for the cleanliness of their streets; the Spaniards, on the contrary, throw before their doors whatever disagreeable objects they are obliged to remove from within. With all the pains taken by the English while in possession of *Monte Video*, and these were great, it was with difficulty the streets could be so cleared as to prevent offence to some of the senses.

The greater part of the time of the inhabitants is spent in religious duties, or in feasting and gambling. Billiard tables are to be met with in every street. Most of them are inclined to an irregular kind of traffic: but the only regular merchants, deserving the appellation, are the Europeans who obtain permission to reside in the province. Many find means of penetrating illegally into the country, where they carry on a contraband trade, in which they receive great encouragement from the natives of the interior.

Great wealth exists in the city and neigh-bourhood; but it does not shew itself in that

magnificence which is so elegantly displayed in
European towns, where not the least proportion
of the means are afforded. The inhabitants are
said to appear to the greatest advantage when
assembled to view the bull-fights exhibited in the
amphitheatre erected for this purpose, and of
which some description has already been given.
These exhibitions took place every Monday afternoon during the summer season, previous to the
invasion under General Beresford, since which
time the Spaniards have become otherwise engaged. At these fights the ladies appeared in
their best attire and richest ornaments: the
principal people occupying boxes whence they
commanded a full view of all the spectators and
of the cruel spectacle. The Vice-roy and his
suite, surrounded by his guards, occupied one
face of the building, over which was hoisted the
Spanish standard: here he sat in all the dignity
which authority could display over a people who
were instructed to humble themselves before rank
and superiority. The bulls, a particularly fierce
breed being reserved for these sports, were com-
batted by a cavalier, and another person on foot,
who had narrow openings made to receive him
from the area in case of being too hard pressed.
Eight thousand spectators could conveniently sit

and view this favorite diversion of the Spaniards. It is not to be doubted but that these exhibitions contribute much towards keeping alive that ferocity of disposition so strongly characteristic of the inferior orders in *Paraguay*, who may be said to exercise it daily in their manner of catching oxen in the plains.

The country people always travel mounted, carrying with them a plaited thong about thirty yards in length, and one inch in circumference, made of the raw hides of oxen. This thong, which is denominated a *lazie*, forms a noose by running through an iron ring of two inches in diameter, at one end; the other is made fast to the saddle: it is gathered in a coil in the left hand, the noose is held in the right. Having fixed on the animal to be secured, he is chased at full gallop, and when a favorable opportunity presents itself the pursuer throws the noose which he has, in the chase, kept whirling round his head, over the bullock's. horns, and seldom misses his cast. The horse, having been well trained to this service, is turned away, and always keeps the thong at full stretch, without straining it too hard, while a second person throws another noose over the beast's rump, which, slipping down, secures him by one of the hind legs, and riding in a contrary

direction to the first, the ox becomes thus secured.
When there is but one person in pursuit, the horse
is taught to stand and keep the bullock firm, while
the rider dismounts and hamstrings him, or cuts
his throat. Nothing could excite greater horror
to us than the indifference with which these
savages committed this slaughter. Besides the
noose, they commonly carry three balls of about
three pounds weight each, suspended to as many
thongs a fathom long, and fastened together at
one end: these they whirl about the head, and
dart with great dexterity at a horse in full
gallop, which encircling his legs, are sure to
throw or stop him. Numbers of these fellows,
with the *lazie,* hovered about us, and managed
to kill or carry off several of our sentinels,
by the use of this noose, dexterously thrown.
Murders are constant among this rabble : no less
than one hundred and six were committed in
Buenos Ayres between January and May last.
In their country excursions, the better sort of
people are obliged to travel armed : but since it
has become necessary to trust every description
of men with fire-arms, the populace do not hold
them so much in dread, and have, in consequence,
become the more insolent. The style of their dress
adds also to their natural ferocious appearance.

Over a black, greasy head of hair, which covers
nearly the whole face, they wear a small hat, not
able to admit the skull, on which it is secured by
a bandage passing under the chin : the throat is
open and bare; the body covered with a short
jacket; and from the waist a loose pair of cotton
drawers descends to the calf of the leg, and over
these a pair of dark breeches, not so long as the
drawers which hang below like a fringe; a knife,
unsheathed, is stuck in a girdle about the waist.
The whole of this dress is covered by a party-
coloured blanket, which falls before and behind,
a slit being made in the middle, to admit the head;
the feet are generally bare. Thus equipped, they
mount their horses, which are in most excellent
training.

If the character of the lower orders is savage
and fierce, it is strongly contrasted by that of the
higher classes, whose conduct towards the British
who fell into their hands, exhibited the highest
civilization and humanity. Those officers of the
71st, who had such opportunities of becoming
thoroughly acquainted with them, spoke of their
hospitality in very high terms. Not the least
injury was offered to those of our wounded who
fell in the streets : they were taken up and carried
into the houses, where the females dressed their

wounds, and shewed them as much attention as they could have done to their own friends, instead of heaping reproaches and insults on those who had entered their peaceable abodes with hostile views. They generally dress after the manner of the Europeans, the elder gentlemen according to the old school, and most of the younger follow the changes of fashion in Europe. The ladies universally wear the peculiar black dress of the *country* in the morning; but in the evening mostly dress after the French costume: they are very fond of ornaments, which are profusely distributed about their heads and elsewhere.

Clerical characters of various orders are to be met with in every part of the town: the Dominicans and Franciscans predominate. Their influence chiefly extends over the most ignorant of the populace, and a few zealots of the better sort: they are, however, in general, not much respected in the town, and their countrymen frequently accused them before the British of licentiousness and debauchery. They pretend to interfere in every transaction, whether civil or military, and during the negociations lost no opportunity of exciting the minds of the armed populace. One example will shew their meddling disposition. On the evening of the 7th, a Dominican monk came to the castle, and with much alarm depicted in his countenance, enquired for General Linier: an *aid-de-camp* of this gentleman's, desired to know the priest's business, who replied that " he came to acquaint him with the " circumstance of the English being employed in " landing heavy ordnance at *El Retiro*," (which was not true) " and requested the alarm to be " sounded in the town." The *aid-de-camp* in his turn informed the priest that " it was no concern " of the monks how the English were employed; " that it was General Linier's business to provide " against circumstances of the kind, and to take " the necessary precautions; and he now would " take this opportunity of telling the informant " that his brethren were taking every little ad-" vantage of the moment to excite tumults among " the mob: and he warned the religious orders " to confine themselves to their monasteries, or " steps would be taken to check such an impudent " interference in public affairs." This determined answer appeared to carry some weight, as their clamours ceased from this moment. It must again be confessed, that there were among these priests, well-informed, sensible, and liberal men.

CHAPTER IX.

Description continued.—Remarks on the Political Disposition of the People, and on the probable Effects of the Invasion to Great Britain *and the American Spaniards.*

I⊤ is not above thirty years since the country on this side the *Cordilleras* was created into a vice-royalty, which also includes some parts of the mountains. The first person who was raised to the dignity of *Vice-roy* attacked the Portuguese possessions in the river, and drove their former possessors farther north, where they have been obliged to confine the boundaries of the *Brazils*, leaving both the banks of the *Plata* in the hands of the Spaniards. There have been nine *vice-roys* since this period. The person holding this high office is President of the Royal Audience, and likewise at the head of the revenue of the province: he is renter of the duties on tobacco, cards, and all other exciseable articles. His salary is stated to be fifty thousand dollars per annum; but his perquisites are far exceeding this amount;

C c

so that he may be said to enjoy a revenue of, at least, thirty thousand pounds sterling. The office of *Vice-roy* of *Paraguay* is generally a prior step to that of *Peru*.

Few mines are found on this side of the *Andes;* but *Buenos Ayres* derives its great wealth from being the intermediate depot for the valuable metals, which are forwarded through it to the mother country, as well as for the merchandize of the latter, for the use of most of her colonies on the south side of the Equator. Though the roads are said to be good on the communications with *Peru* and *Chili*, yet the journies are slowly performed, as the accommodations are bad. There are but few towns beyond *Buenos Ayres;* the principal being *Santa Fé*, situated on the west bank of the *Parana*, a branch of the *Plata*, about two hundred and seventy miles N.W. of the capital; and *Cordova*, about one hundred and fifty westward of *Santa Fé*, said to be next in importance to *Buenos Ayres*. Neither are fortified. Several small villages lie on the roads to these towns. *Colonia del Sacramento* has fallen into entire decay, since the Portuguese have been driven from it; and it will soon be a heap of ruins, unless it should fall into the hands of masters who know the great advantages to be derived from a rich and fertile soil. The French, and other Europeans, settled over the province, speak of it as a perfect garden, but neglected by the occupiers, who alone draw from the earth what she spontaneously sends forth, and her supplies of luxurious fruits and vegetables are bountiful.

The chief command of the troops, and the presidency of the royal audience, was vested, a short time previous to our arrival, in the hands of Linier, a man whose name will be conspicuous in the historical accounts of *South America* at the commencement of the nineteenth century. No man could have better employed the ill-disciplined and heterogeneous army he had assembled together. The civil administration had been entrusted to him but a very few days previous to the attack, the council having sus-pended the *Vice-roy* for his pusillanimous conduct, and for having neglected, through sordid views, the proper preparations for the defence of his province. A Spanish felucca, that had run through our fleet on the morning we landed at *Ensenada*, brought Linier favorable marks of the sense entertained of his conduct by the Spanish Monarch, who confirmed him in the military command, and there is but little doubt of his being rewarded with the *vice-royalty*, for having preserved it from British conquest. Linier is about forty-five years of age, from five feet eight to five feet nine in height, stout, and of a very genteel appearance, with a countenance that bespeaks his generous and noble disposition. In his conversation, he shews the man of the world, and an understanding much improved.

The entrance of the English among the American Spaniards has produced on the minds of the latter a most astonishing effect. It has operated like a flash of lightning; and sensible and well-informed men declare that it has advanced their political ideas above a century, their knowledge of the situation of *Europe* and of their own, as connected with it, being far distantly removed from the truth, it having been the jealous practice of the mother country to keep her colonies in a perfect state of ignorance respecting the transactions on the eastern shores of the *North Atlantic.* They begin to feel their strength, and with it a strong inclination to employ it in an interest more immediately connected with themselves, than what was theirs in the late contest, which only decided upon which of the two European powers they were to be dependent. There are not wanting in *South America* those enterprising characters, who are to be found in all countries, and always ready to take advantage of times of confusion for promoting a revolution, which, in case of success, is sure to advance their fortunes. These men have not let slip so favorable an occasion of advancing their views; and it must likewise be confessed, that many of the respectable inhabitants feel a persuasion that a state of independency would be attended with greater advantages to the population and commerce of the colonies, than in the confined and narrow state in which the ill-judged policy of the mother country restrains them. These sentiments they made no hesitation in openly avowing before the British officers in the Castle, and it is problematical, whether *Buenos Ayres*, and perhaps all *South America*, will not be more irrecoverably lost to the Spanish nation, by the issue of the English invasion, than if it had fallen under our subjugation at this moment. The regular troops in the provinces are very few; and it will become the interest of these to join in the wishes of a people they have not the means of curbing. The maritime force of *Spain* is in too reduced a state to send any armament to check this rising spirit, which must, ere long, create a new independent power in this quarter of the new world.

It is equally a matter of doubt whether *Great Britain* would have benefited so much by the conquest as she may by the emancipation of this country from all foreign subjection. In this latter case, it will be the interest of the American Spaniards to open their ports to all manufacturing nations; for, having none or few manufactures of their own, they will depend entirely upon *Europe* for every article of consumption, with the exception of provisions. *Great Britain*, in the quality and price of her merchandize, protected as is her commerce by a powerful navy, will always command the market of *Buenos Ayres*, through which must pass the supplies to the other provinces. A new channel will be thus opened for circulating the immense stores of our manufactures, which have been accumulating in the merchants' warehouses by the effects of the system pursued on the continent of *Europe* for crippling our trade. In return for our goods we shall obtain the precious metals, or raw materials to be worked at home; so that the benefits of such a commerce are almost incalculable in a moral and political view: for, besides depriving our arch enemies of their chief source of revenue, we shall give ample employment to our fellow-subjects who are reduced to adopt vicious courses for a livelihood. The consumption in *South America* will be sufficient to occupy all our idle hands. Had we conquered the country, a large military force would have been necessary to maintain it; the fertility of the soil and the superiority of the climate would have tempted large emigrations from the British Islands, and the example of the northern states would have been soon followed in the southern colonies depending on *Great Britain*.

It is to be hoped that these few observations will not be considered an improper digression. They are the result of some enquiry, assisted by the reasoning of men acquainted with the commercial interests of *Great Britain*. It is possible, however, that they may not be founded on just speculations.

The Spaniards set a high value on every article from *England:* but this appreciation of our merchandize has suffered, in no trifling degree, by the selfish and fraudulent practices of some traders, who consigned cargoes between the taking of *Buenos Ayres* by General *Beresford*, and the subsequent attack this year. The old rubbish, that had been lying up for years in the warehouses, were shipped off, and disposed of at *Monte Video*, to the country dealers, who, on opening the packages for the retail trade, found the articles not only far inferior to the samples, but, in many instances, totally unfit for use : this was particularly the case with a great part of the hardware, which was in such a state, as almost to be inseparable from the paper the articles were wrapped in, so thickly were they encrusted with rust. Our merchants at *Monte Video* proceeded, likewise, on a principle which they ought to have foreseen would eventually terminate to their disadvantage: they, at first, set a most exorbitant price on their goods, which, as competitors arrived, they were obliged to lower; and being disappointed in an early market at *Buenos Ayres*, the trade became confined within very narrow limits. Many who had embarked their whole credit on this speculation, were obliged to have recourse to public sales for remittances to answer their acceptances at home. The Spaniards, now cautious from former deceptions, became slow in their biddings, and most of the goods, thus disposed of, were purchased at a low value, by those of our own countrymen who sought a monopoly, and could command funds to cover the great expence of waiting for a market at the capital, the probable conquest of which was now approaching. There is no doubt but ruin has been the lot of the greater number of these speculators; and it is lamentable to add, that the morals of the younger part of those entrusted with cargoes have become, by the delays occasioned them, as desperate as their fortunes. They constantly filled the gambling houses of *Monte Video*, and their time was there spent in dissipation and extravagance.

The great staple commodities of this province are hides and tallow, obtained from the great droves of cattle covering the extensive plains. These cattle are not the property of whoever chooses to hunt them, but belong to individuals, who have their private mark on them. At a particular season, the herdsmen and slaves drive into enclosures, made for the purpose, the cows, with their young, the former having the owner's mark: the male calves are gelded, and the whole receive the impression by which they are afterwards distinguished; they then range at liberty until killed for their skins and fat. The first are stretched by stakes driven into the ground; the sun dries them, and they are then doubled for exportation; many are cut up into thongs, which are substituted, in almost every instance, where cordage is elsewhere applied. Those hides, in which the tallow is packed, are suspended, while green, by the four corners, to as many poles, and weights attached to draw it down,

D d

thus forming a case without seams; in this the warm fat is poured, the ends of the hide are then folded over, and one of the best packages is made for such an article across the torrid zone. Great numbers of hogs range the plains; but their meat is not sought after, as it is considered unwholesome from their feeding so much on the animal substances afforded by the great mortality among the cattle. The dogs are likewise found in a wild state, collected in large bodies over the plains: these, as well as the tygers inhabiting the thickets which border the greater streams flowing into the *Plata*, commit great havock on the horned animals. The wool of the sheep is coarse, and not very fit for purposes of trade, and their flesh is only prepared for the slaves. There was in the public stores, at *Buenos Ayres*, a rich collection of the finer wool, from the mountains, which would have fallen into the hands of the army, had it been successful, as also quicksilver and Peruvian bark to an immense amount.

CHAPTER X.

Thanks returned to the Army in General Orders.—Disorders arising from the Fatigues of the Army.—Arrival, at Monte Video, *of the Spanish Hostages, also of the* 89th Infantry.—Proclamation, and Remarks thereon.—Departure of the First Division for* England.

Some few days after our return to *Monte Video*, the General Commanding the Forces returned thanks, in public orders, to the army, for the patience with which they had borne a tedious and fatiguing march, and for the spirit and gallantry displayed by every individual corps when brought into action. A general court-martial was ordered to assemble, for the trial of the infamous characters who had so basely deserted to the Spanish standard, at the moment the bodies of their slaughtered comrades strewed the streets. Above fifty of these wretches had been given up by Linier, to the great satisfaction of the whole army, the British prisoners having met with more insolence and abuse from their countrymen serving with the Spaniards, when we entered the town, than from the country rabble. The railings and scurrility of these vagabonds, particularly towards the officers, gave offence to the very Spaniards.

The hardships which had been endured, now broke out in disorders among the troops. Dysenteries and fevers were encreasing to that degree, as to crowd all the hospital ships, the hospital on shore being appropriated for the wounded, who, in general, were doing very well. Sir Samuel Auchmuty's army had suffered much, also, on their arrival in the country, from the same disorders, but which had originated from different causes to what had occasioned them among the troops serving against *Buenos Ayres*. He had arrived at a time when all the trees were loaded with unripe fruit, from the use of which it was impossible to prevent the soldier, who seldom considers how dearly he may pay at a future period for a present gratification. The troops were, likewise, exposed to the summer heat of the day, and heavy dews of the night: and the medical gentlemen were very unfortunate in the treatment of the wounded at *Monte Video*, a greater number having died than their cases would have originally given reason to expect.

The Saracen sloop of war had sailed for *England*, with dispatches, on the 10th of July: Brigadiers Sir Samuel Auchmuty and Craufurd went home in her. Preparations were now making for the departure of the troops for *England* who could not take any active part in the war before their return : these were, the light brigade, composed of the Rifle Corps and the light companies, and the 88th Regiment. The 47th and 87th Regiments were completed with draughts from the different corps, and sailed, on the 1st of August, for the *Cape of Good Hope*, whence they were to be conveyed to *India*.

It was not until the 22d of July, that we obtained any intelligence of the detachments under Brigadier-General Auckland, and for whose safety we were under serious apprehensions, as it was now above twenty weeks since they had left *England*. It was the 24th before some of this convoy entered the harbour of *Monte Video*, and several days more elapsed before the whole were in : they had met with severe weather on the passage, and, at the time of their arrival, were in possession of but one week's provisions. One vessel, that had left the *Thames* so late as the 29th of May, came in with them.

The Spanish hostages, for the fulfilment of the

convention, came down to *Monte Video* on the 31st of July, and attended with a very numerous suite. Ours had been left at *Buenos Ayres* before the reimbarkation, and consisted of three captains. The Spaniards gave us men of rank; and among them was Colonel *Ellio*, who was the officer commanding the divisions routed by Colonel Pack, at *St. Pedro*, on the 7th of June, and was to succeed to the command of *Monte Video*. To the disgust of the army, this man was allowed to assume functions as commander, issuing proclamations, and doing other acts of authority.

On the morning of the entry of these Spaniards our Commander in Chief issued a proclamation, in which he expressed himself as having learnt that opinions were entertained by the English merchants and others, tending to question the good faith of the British nation in respect to the late treaty; and that under such delusion, those interested, might not take the necessary measures for quitting *Monte Video* at the same time with the troops, in the expectation that the evacuation would not take place: the proclamation therefore warned all English residents to have their property ready for embarkation, as such as would not be prepared to sail out of the harbour on the 6th of September should be considered out of the pro-

tection of the British force. So little possible was
it to reconcile the late events by any reasoning
on the circumstances which led to them, that it
cannot excite surprize that doubts should be
entertained respecting the real intentions of those
at the head of our government in *South America;*
and less surprize will be felt at finding the
expectations of the traders so congenial to their
interests; for, carrying into effect the terms of
the convention consigned them to ruin, from
which a renewal of hostilities could alone preserve
them.   The troops may be conceived equally
anxious to have an opportunity of re-commencing
the contest, although filled with every sentiment
respecting their commanders, but such as soldiers
should entertain of their chiefs. When joined
by the 89th Infantry, they were competent to
conquering and retaining possession of the vice-
royalty, under generals possessing the proper
qualifications for such a command. As to the
Spaniards, they were too well aware of the very
great advantages they had obtained by the treaty
to run the hazard of losing them by the least
deviation which could be construed into an
offence.

It would not be fair to deduce the attentions
shewn by General Liniers to the English hostages

and wounded left at *Buenos Ayres*, from such a motive alone as that of policy. His character had already been too well established for gene-rosity and humanity, not to suppose him actuated chiefly by these, which equally predominated in the conduct of almost every decent Spaniard. Those officers whose recovery was sufficiently advanced, were sent down to join their regiments at *Monte Video*, where they arrived filled with encomiums on the hospitable treatment they had met with. It is but justice to add, that these attentions only ceased when the ground covered the remains of such of their guests as died of their wounds, and they were not few. Among others, Colonel Kington, of the 6th Dragoon Guards, fell a victim to a lock-jaw, the conse-quence of a wound in the leg. His corpse was attended to the grave by the Spanish General, the municipality and gentry of the place, a battalion paying military honors on the melancholy occasion.

While the first division destined to return home was preparing for its departure, we underwent some severe gales, accompanied at times with heavy thunder and rain: the harbour was strongly affected on these occasions, the ships being one day two or three feet buried in the mud, and shortly after having as much water to spare,

On the 8th of August, the transports, having
on board the 9th and 20th Light Dragoons, the
Rifle Corps, and 88th Regiment, got under weigh,
and stood up the river to take in fresh water for
the homeward-bound voyage. This was effected
on the 10th, when about thirty miles above *Monte
Video*. We weighed the next day to proceed on our
voyage homeward, under convoy of the Unicorn
and Thisbe frigates: their charge consisted of
seventeen sail. The fleet was obliged to anchor
again in the evening; but on the 12th we finally
took up our anchor, and stood down the river with a
very fresh breeze from the S.W. accompanied with
thick weather, in which the Alexander transport,
with some of the Rifle Corps on board, parted
from us.

The wind continued to blow fresh from the
southward and westward until the 16th, when it
came round to the N.N.W. and north points, from
which it blew for a week, bringing with it incessant
rains. Having in this time attained about the 32°
of lat. and in long. 34°, the wind again came from
the S.W. and we stood our course to the N.E.

Owing to the variation of the winds, which,
however, chiefly prevailed in the N.E. we did not
get sight of *Trinidada* before the 31st, and were
obliged to pass to leeward of it. Contrary to

E e

our expectations, in these latitudes, we were baffled by a N.E. and N.N.E. wind; so that when in 13° of lat. and in long. 31° 34', finding no chance of making any progress in this direction, we put about, and went in search of the S.E. trade, more to the southward and eastward. Having passed, on the 6th of September, between *Trinidad* and the small islands of *Martin Vaz*, we fell in, on the 8th, with the desired wind from the S.E. and then stood to the N.N.E. We had, by this time, run back as far as 21° 07' lat. and long. 27° 23'. Favored by the weather, we crossed the Equator on the 20th of September, in long. 23°, and were fortunate enough to have a continuance of the S.E. breeze until attaining the 8th degree of north latitude, when the airs became light and baffling, afterwards settling into a calm. We attributed the circumstance of not meeting this before, to our having encountered the sun near the line, as he had only 59' of north declination on the day we passed it.

On the 1st of October, the appearances of the weather denoted the approach to the trade wind; and on the 2d it settled in the N.E. and blew between this and the east points until we had attained about the 26th degree of latitude on the 12th, and our course had carried us as far as

34° west longitude; when the airs became light and unsettled. On this day the wind blew from the S.S.E. and pretty fresh, but it again died away.

We now experienced great benefits from the precautions taken by General Craufurd before quitting *England*, either to prevent disease, or to remedy it in case of its appearance in his army. The scurvy began to break out among the troops, and more particularly on board of the men of war, where it bore serious symptoms. Had it not been for the ample provision of lime-juice, found on board those transports which had originally formed part of General Craufurd's expedition, the troops must at this time have suffered considerably, as all the other ships were unprovided with a supply of this article, so valuable on long voyages. It was, however, to be lamented, that, owing to fraud on the part of some of those persons through whose hands this acid had passed, it was found, on issuing it, to be much adulterated; so much so, in some cases, that no sign remained by which it could be proved that the juice of the lime had ever entered into the composition issued as such; consequently, its effects could not be so certainly relied on as if it had been genuine.

On the 16th of the month, we had only attained the 29° of latitude, when a breeze sprung up from the southward. It freshened, and carried us, at a brisk rate, on a course which, allowing for variation, was due north, as it was intended to go to the westward of the *Azores*. Our progress was much impeded by some wooden-bottomed ships, which frequently occasioned the fleet to lay-to. The rains were now very heavy.

In the afternoon of Sunday, the 18th, when in lat. 34° 30′, a most violent squall suddenly attacked the convoy, when sailing under a press of canvass, with a breeze aft. It came chiefly from the north-west, although it veered completely round the compass. Such was its violence, and so little prepared were we for it, that there was scarcely one vessel that did not suffer some loss in her sails. We had six destroyed in our ship; our fore-top sail, and main-top-gallant sail, were actually scattered about the ship like the fragments of torn paper. One vessel, about a half-mile from us, had not a single sail left to her yards, and we observed another with her main yard carried away. Fortunately, this gust did not hold with an equal degree of fury for above twenty minutes, although it continued to blow severely for an hour after, accompanied with heavy rain, thunder, and 'lightning. The wind again settled in the east; and the next morning we could see but two more of the convoy, when the momentary cessations of thick weather gave us a more extensive horizon. The wind now encreased to a gale from the S.S.E. until the morning of the 23d, when it moderated and cleared up.

On this day we had been carried with nothing but a reefed fore-top sail and storm stay sail set, into 43° 47′ north lat. and were by our reckoning in 34° 50′ W. long. when, having parted convoy about twenty-four hours, we opened our secret instructions, which directed us to repair to *Spithead.* We accordingly altered our course to E. N. E. with the wind in the old quarter: and likewise put ourselves in a state of defence against any insults from privateers.

On the 27th we fell in with His Majesty's ship Buffalo, from *New South Wales*, but last from *Rio Janiero*, which she had left so far back as the 12th of August, the same day we passed *Monte Video*, homeward bound. The next day we joined two more of our fleet, and the Buffalo took us under her convoy.

The wind coming favorable on the 29th, we stood to the eastward, and on the 1st of November fell in with the Thisbe, and learnt from her that the convoy was a-head. She took the Ceres in charge, as this transport was a very dull sailer, and we continued on with the Buffalo: the James and Rebecca likewise managed to keep up with us.

On the 5th we sounded and got bottom with eighty fathoms. Standing up *Channel*, the Buffalo the next afternoon made the signal for land, but the weather getting very thick, we could not plainly distinguish it, but supposed it to be *Scilly*. It blew very hard during the night, when we parted from the Buffalo; and the James and Rebecca ran ashore in *Mounts Bay*, at the back of the *Lizard*, where she was totally wrecked, and twenty-six soldiers, ten seamen, and two children lost : the remainder escaped on shore through the humane assistance they received from the inhabitants of the neighbourhood.

We rejoined the Buffalo on the 7th, and on Sunday, the 8th, came to anchor at *Spithead*, where we found the Unicorn and Thisbe frigates, with a part of the convoy. Among them was the Alexander, which had on board a part of the Rifle Corps, and which had parted company on quitting the *Rio de la Plata :* she had steered directly for *England*, where she arrived a week before us without having met with any particular interruption on her passage. The whole convoy entered some of the ports of the *Channel* a few days after us, with the exception of the Alexander hospital-ship. for whose safety there is every reason to be apprehensive, as she was never met with after the gale off the *Azores*, and her condition was such as to render her barely capable of supporting its fury. The only hope left for the preservation of those on board is that she may have been carried into an enemy's port. She had embarked in her about eighty wounded men, besides a small detachment of the 88th to work her pumps. There were likewise passengers in her, the widows of some of the officers killed at *Buenos Ayres*, and several medical gentlemen.

We found also at anchor at *Spithead*, the Medusa frigate, that had arrived the day before us, with Lieutenant-General Whitelocke and staff. She had left *Monte Video* with the remaining division of the transports and merchantmen on the 9th of September, on which day the evacuation was carried into effect, which had been prevented on the 7th and 8th by the bad weather. The fleet had gone up to water, and then stood down the river, of which they had got clear on the 12th, when the Medusa left them. They were to touch at *St. Helena* for refreshments, and then continue their course home, so that they may be expected about the beginning of next January.

THE END.

Printed by G. E. Miles,
127, *Oxford Street.*

Lightning Source UK Ltd.
Milton Keynes UK
UKOW07f0006170216

268531UK00007B/213/P